Juliet's Answer

Juliet's Answer

One Man's Search for Love
and the Elusive Cure for Heartbreak

GLENN DIXON

G

GALLERY BOOKS

New York   London   Toronto   Sydney   New Delhi

G

Gallery Books
An Imprint of Simon & Schuster, Inc.
1230 Avenue of the Americas
New York, NY 10020

First Gallery Books trade paperback edition February 2017

GALLERY BOOKS and colophon are registered trademarks of Simon & Schuster, Inc.

For information about special discounts for bulk purchases, please contact Simon & Schuster Special Sales at 1-866-506-1949 or business@simonandschuster.com.

Verona map design by Tony Hanyk, tonyhanyk.com.

The Simon & Schuster Speakers Bureau can bring authors to your live event. For more information or to book an event contact the Simon & Schuster Speakers Bureau at 1-866-248-3049 or visit our website at www.simonspeakers.com.

Interior design by Lewelin Polanco
Verona map design by Tony Hanyk, tonyhanyk.com.

Manufactured in the United States of America

10 9 8 7 6 5 4 3 2 1

Library of Congress Cataloging-in-Publication Data

ISBN 978-1-5011-4185-0
ISBN 978-1-5011-4186-7 (ebook)

For Mom and Dad,
who have been together now
for sixty-two years

Juliet's Answer

1. CASA DI GIULIETTA—THE HOUSE OF JULIET
2. ARENA DI VERONA—THE ANCIENT ROMAN ARENA
3. PONTE NUOVO—THE "NEW BRIDGE," CONSTRUCTED 1334
4. NUMBER 3, VIA GALILEO GALILEI—OLD OFFICES OF THE CLUB DI GIULIETTA
5. CIMITERO MONUMENTALE—VERONA CITY CEMETERY
6. CORSO PORTA BORSARI
7. VICOLO SANTA CECILIA
8. FIUME ADIGE—THE ADIGE RIVER
9. GELATERIA SAVOIA
10. TOMBA DI GIULIETTA—JULIET'S TOMB
11. PIAZZA DELLE ERBE—VEGETABLE MARKET
12. PORTA LEONI—THE GATE OF LIONS
13. "CASA DI ROMEO"—ROMEO'S HOUSE
14. TOMBA DI CANGRANDE DELLA SCALA—TOMB OF PRINCE ESCALUS
15. NUMBER 7, VIA DEI MONTECCHI—GLENN'S HOTEL, POSSIBLE TRUE HOME OF THE MONTAGUES
16. CASTELVECCHIO
17. BASILICA DI SAN ZENO MAGGIORE
18. PIZZERIA LEON D'ORO
19. TORRE DEI LAMBERTI—THE LAMBERTI TOWER

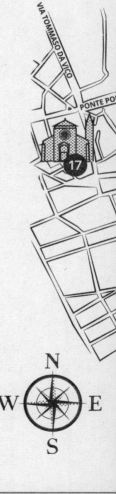

A MAP OF OLD
VERONA

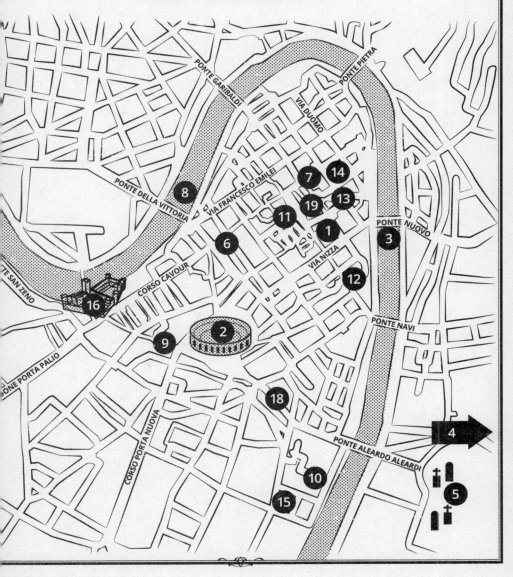

A Note to the Reader

A tiny office in Verona, Italy, receives more than ten thousand letters a year, all of them addressed to Juliet, the fictional character in Shakespeare's tragic play *Romeo and Juliet*. The letters speak of heartbreak and the endless search for love. They come from all over the world, and every letter is answered by a group of women calling themselves "the secretaries of Juliet." They have been answering letters for decades. There are those who believe that *Romeo and Juliet* is actually a true story of star-crossed lovers who lived in Verona in the year 1302. We may never know the truth, but the figure of young Juliet lives on as the symbol of a once-perfect love.

Contents

Act One

In fair Verona, where we lay our scene

Dear Juliet,

I am no longer young, but there was a time, yes, there was a time when I believed in love. I can sound out the names of lovers and draw up their faces, each one, so clearly. And then they are gone. Why is it that love comes so easily for some but refuses to stay for others? Why should it be so? Why should it twist our souls so grievously?

I read the letter all the way through. It looked like the others in the pile, nothing terribly special about it. These letters are all handwritten—matters so close to the heart cannot be typed—then they are folded into hopeful envelopes and mailed to Juliet, care of Verona.

Giovanna appeared at my door. *"Ciao,"* she said. "Would you care for a coffee?"

"No, I . . . I'm okay."

Giovanna wore pearls even in the afternoon. She swept into the room, glanced at the letter in front of me, and read my thoughts. "Some are quite moving, are they not?"

"I'm not sure how to answer this one."

"Ah," she said, scraping a wooden chair in to sit beside me. She bent over the letter, tipping her reading glasses slightly. "Many of the letters are full of sadness. They are poetry too sometimes."

"So how should I answer?"

She peered at me. "Sometimes it is enough for them just to write."

"This woman writes so beautifully. I'm not sure I—"

"The answer," she went on, patting the letter, "is often contained in their words."

"But—"

"You must be like a fortune-teller. You must watch for signs. The writer will tell you what they want to hear."

"I don't know."

Giovanna looked at me as if I were slow. "She needs to know that her life is good, that she is worthy, that she is important. She needs to know that. That's what you must write."

"And then I sign it 'Juliet'?"

"If you wish. Or you can sign 'Juliet's secretary.'"

"Okay."

Giovanna stood and straightened her dress. "We take this responsibility very seriously." She turned on her heels and walked to the doorway, where she hovered, a slender hand on the doorframe.

"Yes, of course," I said.

"No coffee then?" She fixed me with a final stare.

"No, thanks. I'll just get to work."

"Va bene." She lingered, watching, then brushed out of the room.

———

There is no Juliet, of course, though the tourist board of Verona would certainly like you to believe there is. Verona is an ancient city. Around it lie the fields of Valpolicella, valley of the cellars, some of the oldest vineyards in the world. Julius Caesar spent his summers here. Dante came in exile to finish his *Divine Comedy*. But nothing is as singular to the city as the legend of Romeo and Juliet.

When I first crossed into the old town, I passed through a gate in the towering medieval walls. On a bronze plaque there, bolted to the stones, were the words THERE IS NO WORLD WITHOUT VERONA WALLS, BUT PURGATORY, TORTURE, HELL ITSELF.

That was Romeo's line. He didn't exist either, at least not exactly.

Plaques like these are all over Verona, marking the major events in Shakespeare's play—a story that was not written here, a story that was made famous centuries before, in a different language and a different country.

I arrived in Verona at the end of July, two years ago, with a pock-etful of questions. I was here to learn something. Something about love and maybe something about Shakespeare. Already I could see the crowds ahead of me, bunching and yammering, cameras at the ready, and I knew exactly where they were headed. The throngs funneled past gleaming shopwindows, past the cashmere sweaters and five-hundred-dollar shoes on display, and I was swept along with them. The street opened into a square on our left, but the crowd veered right and then, suddenly, there was an arch and a passageway before us and a sign that read CASA DI GIULIETTA—the House of Juliet. Here we were at last. We grew silent and reverent. I'll admit I was cynical. Many of the younger women were enraptured, dragging along boyfriends desperately feigning interest. "It's not real!" I wanted to call out. "It's just a story!"

We shuffled under a stone archway and emerged into a courtyard. And there it was: the famous balcony. It jutted from the wall, ten feet above us. Vines, perfect for climbing, tangled up the old stones. It was a little too perfect. The balcony itself is actually an ancient Roman sarcophagus. It was incorporated into the wall in 1937 to lure gullible tourists like us. You can go inside the house too—it's a sort of museum—and various young lovers come out on the balcony to get their photographs taken. Below, crowds cheer when they kiss. Cameras click. Texts are sent.

By the steps to the entrance, a placard tells the history of the house. I squeezed through the crowd to get close enough to read it: THIS HOUSE, it said, HAS BEEN IN THE POSSESSION OF ONE FAMILY SINCE THE THIRTEENTH CENTURY. Above the arch is their emblem, the insignia of the Cappello family—a rounded hat like a bowler, as the Cappellos were, apparently, hatmakers.

Now, that surprised me. The Capulet name was obviously derived from Cappello. How would Shakespeare have known that? I looked around. Had he been here? There are lost years in his life—years when he may have been traveling overseas, but it's not generally believed that he ever made it to Verona. The answer is simpler, as most answers are. Shakespeare almost certainly adapted *Romeo and Juliet* from an earlier work, and that work—an epic poem—had in turn been adapted from an Italian story dating back to around 1530.

This old courtyard, then, has been a place of pilgrimage for at least two hundred years. Charles Dickens came to see it and write about it. He didn't like it much. The house had degenerated at that time into a miserable little inn with a brutish dog at the door and geese waddling across the courtyard. Now it flapped with tourists. Dickens probably wouldn't have liked that either. In one corner stands a bronze statue of Juliet, her eyes cast downward, demure, her long fingers self-consciously clasping the folds of her diaphanous gown.

For reasons I don't completely understand, you are supposed to gently cup your hand over her right breast and make your wish to the gods of love. One by one, the pilgrims step up to fondle her breast.

The bronze there is polished to a golden sheen. Her face, meanwhile, is darkened with a charcoal patina.

For some time, I watched the crowds, until I noticed an elderly woman strolling the yard in contemplation. She moved from one feature to another, lingering at each, reading the placards, standing before the statue and then, just before leaving, she hesitated. She turned to take in the balcony one last time, then nodded before disappearing under the stones of the archway. And where the woman had been standing, a bright red wooden letter box appeared. I hadn't noticed it until that moment. It was hand-tooled, intricate in its carpentry, painted crimson, and mounted on the brick wall by the entrance to the house. I edged over to it. POSTA DI GIULIETTA, it read. Letters to Juliet.

———

When letters to Juliet started arriving in Verona in 1937, no one knew what to do with them. They were propped up against the gravestones at the Monastery of San Francesco, long said to be the home of Juliet's vault, and the groundskeeper there took it upon himself to answer them. By the '50s, a poet had taken over the task, and by 1989, a baker named Giulio Tamassia had stepped in to answer the steady flow of letters. Giulio eventually retired from the confectionery business and opened up the first official office for the letters to Juliet. Hundreds of them were pouring in to Verona by this point, and Giulio set himself to the task of answering—for the next twenty-five years.

Giovanna, Giulio Tamassia's daughter, took over the operations from her father and now manages the Club di Giulietta, whose staff sort the letters into languages, answer them, and then catalogue the originals. Giovanna complains that the city is not paying them enough to cover their postage, that they don't help with the rent on the office, but still the letters flood in, overflowing boxes and spilling off counters.

I'd e-mailed Giovanna months before to ask if I could come to

Verona and volunteer to answer letters to Juliet. Of course, my motives went deeper. I had a situation of my own that I was trying to figure out, but that's not what I told Giovanna. I was a writer, I said. I'd been a teacher for a long time. I'd taught *Romeo and Juliet* and maybe I could help with the letters—the English letters, at least.

The day I arrived, she picked me up at my hotel—barely an hour after I'd clumped up from the train station. She parked nearby and strode up the sidewalk to where I was waiting.

"You are Glenn Dixon?"

"Giovanna?"

"Yes. Come, I am on my way to the office now."

She didn't say much. I wondered if she had seen this all before—if it was quite common for foreign volunteers to show up, earnest and eager, but maybe not up to the task. I wondered if this was all really a bit of a bother to her.

"Here is the Roman arena," she said at one point, breaking the silence, looking out the windshield at the wide piazza in front of us.

"Okay," I said, but I was too new to the city to know what she was talking about. I sat rigid in the passenger seat and we turned right, under medieval battlements the color of burnt umber. We crossed a bridge, the Ponte Nuovo, skirted a cemetery, and then wound down into an industrial area of offices and warehouses. At number 3, Via Galileo Galilei, we pulled in. A blue bicycle was tipped against the wall and the front door was propped open. Inside, it looked just like any other office reception room, with a potted plant and a front counter that faced the door.

Giovanna waved me in and pointed to a chair at a round table just in front of the counter. She sat down beside me and began to talk. First, she spoke about her father—he's still alive—and I asked her a bit more about the history of the place.

"It is a long story," she said, glancing back at the counter and the piles of paperwork there.

"But it all happens here. All the letters are answered here?" I pressed.

"Yes, of course. We are very busy."

The place was in a state of organized frenzy. Opera posters and framed photographs obscured the walls. Books and papers lined the counters, tall and squared, like military squadrons ready to tumble. "So," I said, "how many letters do you get a month?"

"Come," she said, rising abruptly. I trailed her down a corridor to a smaller office at the back. *Office* is a euphemism. It was more like a warehouse. Shelves ran along two of the walls, sagging under the weight of a dozen or so cardboard boxes. All of the boxes brimmed with letters, and each was labeled according to language: Russian, Chinese, Swedish, French. Along the third wall was a counter with chairs pulled up to it as a sort of makeshift desk. An English box had already been placed there. Someone had set up a little workstation for me with a stack of stationery and envelopes. They'd even laid a pen out, just so, parallel to the papers.

"It will take some time for you to read them all," Giovanna said, pointing at the box. There were several hundred letters in just this one box. Maybe even a thousand. My smile faded.

I scooped up a handful of letters. Many were in pale violet or thick, creamy envelopes, as if they were wedding invitations. But there were also loose scraps of paper, letters hastily written and, I imagined, dumped at the last minute into the letter box at Juliet's house. I picked up one that was simply scrawled on the back of a train ticket. The return address: Brazil. I dropped it back into the box.

"Would you like to begin now?" Giovanna asked. "You can sit here."

I did as I was told. It was going to be a long afternoon.

"Write your answers on these," she said, tapping the stack of four-by-six sheets she'd left for me. "Then tuck them into the envelopes—but do not seal them."

I looked at the return envelopes. They were printed with a graphic of Juliet on the balcony. Her hair was whipping in the wind, her hand outstretched imploringly. She looked more like a pinup girl from the 1950s than anything from Shakespeare.

"I will be out front if you have any questions." She eyed me for a moment, then swept out of the office more quickly than I would have liked. I thought there'd be a little more in-service, maybe some training. I wasn't sure I was ready.

I heaved the English box a little closer and the letters within shifted like sand. A few slid onto the counter and I reached for the nearest one. The letter was from the United States—California. I opened the envelope and began to read: "George left us on April 7, 2014. He and I were married for twenty-five years."

Ah. A tragic tale of loss. But then I kept reading.

"I have recently met again with an old love of mine, Harry. Is it too soon? Is it too soon to feel these feelings again?"

What could I say to that? I didn't even know Harry.

I pushed back my chair, ready to call Giovanna, but thought better of it. How could I admit defeat on the first letter? I read the letter all the way to the end, paused, then picked up a pen and paper.

"Dear Jane," I wrote. "You will find the answer in your heart."

I looked down at my page. What a load of bunk. I balled up the sheet and began again. I wrote another trite cliché, reread it, then crumpled up that answer too. I dropped Jane's letter back into the box.

Maybe that was just a hard one. I needed to start off easier, something that wasn't so complicated. I plucked another from the pile.

Dear Juliet,

I have been excepted [sic] into a university far away from where I live. It's a very good university and a very good opportunity for me.

The only thing is, I have just met a guy. He lives here. Please, what should I do?

Ha, I thought, I can answer that. I thanked her for her letter, then urged her to go on to university. I told her that the guy would wait for her—if he was worth anything at all. Then I added Polonius's line from *Hamlet*: "To thine own self be true." I thought that sounded good. I put my reply in an envelope and picked up the next letter.

"Dear Juliet," it read. "I am sixteen years old. I have waited for so long to meet my Romeo. When will he appear?" *Oh, honey. You're sixteen. You have a whole world of pain ahead of you. Don't worry.* I didn't write that. Instead, I wrote that she should be patient. That she should go and do the things she loved to do and that she might then find her love engaged in similar pursuits—and wouldn't that be perfect?

Letter by letter, response by response, I fell into a rhythm. Each answer was two or three paragraphs long. I made sure to offer lots of reassurance that love would come, even if it had been lost. I used the "To thine own self be true" line embarrassingly often. As I wrote, I imagined writing letters to my younger self. It helped me with the answers, though truthfully, most of the time I felt like a high school guidance counselor, doling out advice that was likely irrelevant.

For the rest of the morning, I answered letters—thirty maybe—and read many more. The letters were mostly from the UK, the U.S., and my home, Canada. I answered letters from as far away as China, India, Mexico, and Poland. Sometimes the English was broken and simple, but the sentiments were all the same. All of them were asking about love. All were asking about this soul-wrenching experience that is both our deepest sorrow and our greatest joy.

———

I'd had my own problems in love. And part of the reason I had come to Verona was to learn something more about this all-encompassing

11

force in our lives. To learn something, anything, that would help me understand my own heartbreak and help me, maybe, trust in love once more.

Until relatively recently, romantic love was thought to be a cultural construct. The idea of romantic love arose, allegedly, in the early Middle Ages, probably in France. It came to us through the etiquettes of courtly love, immortalized in the songs of troubadours and in the mores of chivalry.

Of course, that's not quite right. Love has been around for much longer than we can imagine. And it's not particular to any one culture. Everyone everywhere experiences love. No one had to invent it. In a recent study across fifteen thousand people in forty-eight countries, romantic love appeared in every culture. It's now believed to be among two hundred universally human traits—like the ability to use language to communicate, or to create and enjoy music, or the presence of laughter. Scientists actually keep track of this sort of thing. The ability to love, it seems, is central to being human.

We all feel attraction to others, something that goes beyond sexual desire. In one study, five-year-olds reported being in love just as frequently as eighteen-year-olds, and it wasn't their teddy bears they were talking about. The children had all the symptoms of adults—butterflies in the stomach, a helpless yearning, and an overwhelming need to be noticed by the object of their affections.

I certainly remember my first love. When Shannon Mahoney appeared at the door to Mrs. Acton's grade-seven math class, I was completely smitten. I don't know why. I just remember that it was instantaneous. She was thirteen, I was twelve, and for the next two years I was madly in love with her—though I don't think I ever said more than, "Could you please pass the pencil crayons?" to this earthly angel. I dreamed up all sorts of fantasies about her, mostly elaborate escapades where I'd rescue her from distress, scenarios that usually involved water, because I was a really good swimmer.

And then one day, my feelings suddenly faded away.

Why any of this should be is not well understood. Why is it that I fell for that one girl in particular? Why Shannon Mahoney? Why did I fixate on her above all the other girls in my junior high school? Was it pheromones? Was it how she looked? Was it something about our particular genetic makeup? What the hell was it?

As I sat reading letter after letter at that counter in Verona, decades and numerous heartbreaks after the unforgettable Shannon Mahoney, I was struck by the fact that so many people were asking versions of these same questions, all wanting to know from "Juliet," this supposed paragon of romantic wisdom, how love worked. Some of the letters spoke of the pinnacles of happiness and joy, the high points of love. One woman wrote that she was in Verona on her honeymoon. "Thank you, Juliet," she gushed. "Thank you, thank you, thank you!" Others—I would say the majority of the letters—seared with the agony of rejection. "Why?" they asked. "Why is this happening to me?"

"Your time will come," I wrote again and again. But I wasn't sure that was true. My time had never come. Often I felt like an imposter and a cheat as I wrote "Juliet's" answers. When I thought about my own life, I knew full well that I hadn't fared well in the game of love. I was as lost as any of these sad hearts, and, really, who was I to advise them? Who was I to tell them anything about love?

The phone rang in the main office. Giovanna answered and spoke in Italian. I couldn't understand anything she was saying. She sounded a little exasperated, and a few moments later, she appeared at my door.

"The Korean Broadcasting System has telephoned."

"The Korean . . . what?"

"They're bringing a camera crew here."

"What? Now?" I put down my pen.

"Yes. In fifteen minutes. They want to film what we do here."

"Okay."

"Va bene," she said. "You will be on camera." She whirled and disappeared down the hall.

I was promoted to the front office before the camera crew arrived. Giovanna called out to two of the other secretaries—both young women—and gathered us around the front table so that we looked like an ad hoc book club. When the Korean Broadcasting System arrived, there were only two of them, with a small handheld video camera between them. I immediately felt suspicious: Korean Broadcasting System, my ass. These guys looked like they were making a YouTube video.

The taller of the two seemed to be in charge. He bounced in, speaking flawless Italian, which caught all of us off guard. He held the camera in one hand and floated around the table taking swooping shots, hovering over us as we wrote letters with wobbling pens in hand. The second man was shorter. He stayed in the background and didn't say much. I don't think he understood Italian. He hummed a lot and spoke in short sentences—in Korean—to the guy with the camera.

"Hmm," the shorter guy said, eyeing me, as if he'd just had a thought. He said something to the taller one, and the camera wheeled around to hover in front of my face.

"What you do here?" the taller guy asked from behind the tiny camera lens. Giovanna had already explained that I was a volunteer from Canada. The red light was blinking expectantly in my face.

"You mean why have I come here, to Verona?"

"Yes, why?"

"To answer the English letters to Juliet. I used to be a teacher. I taught *Romeo and Juliet*, so . . ."

"Teacher. Yes, you are teacher?"

"I *was*, but now I'm here. And I'm just . . . interested in learning something about love."

14

"You know love?"

"Um. I know something. I hope."

"You like love?"

This was going nowhere. I turned to Giovanna and she spoke to the man in Italian. The camera swiveled her way and they launched into an extended interview. Halfway through, Giovanna dismissed the rest of us and I fled back to my little back office and the rows of cardboard boxes.

Half an hour later, the shorter of the two men poked his head in at me.

"Hello," I said.

"I understand you are interested in learning about love," he said. He spoke in almost perfect English.

"Um, yes." I pushed back my chair. "That's the idea."

"Very interesting."

There was a pause. I wasn't sure what to say. "Listen, are you guys really with the Korean Broadcasting System?"

"Yes," he said, or rather, hummed. "I am the producer for this show. And the host. Every week we feature a different city around the world. We are doing Verona now."

"You're the host?"

"Yes. I don't speak Italian, so Hyun-ki is my handler here. My show is called *Backpack Travels*. This episode will air at the end of September."

"All across Korea?"

"KBS Global, yes." He was looking past me now at the piles of letters spread across the counter. "Hmmm. Do you have any letters from Korea?"

"I think so," I said. "But the letter I have is written in English."

"Many Korean people speak English," he said.

I fished through the papers in front of me. I'd been pulling out scores of letters, ten at a time. I had some notes of research too. Papers lay in mountains around me. "Here," I said, holding out a plain white sheet of paper. The paper crinkled and rustled as he smoothed it against the counter. Out front, the handler was chattering away to Giovanna.

"What does it say?" I asked.

"It is a familiar Korean problem."

"What is 'a familiar Korean problem'?"

He lowered the paper. "A two-culture problem. She is fighting with her father about who she should marry. The younger generation wants to be like you Americans."

"Canadian."

"Same thing."

"Not really, but okay."

"Young people in my country want to marry for love. The father wants a marriage between two families."

"An arranged marriage?"

"No, not exactly. But not a marriage strictly for love either. A marriage for the family. A marriage for business. For many reasons."

"Oh," I said.

"Listen," he went on, reading out loud: "'I tried saying I love you once and my dad said, "What are you, American now? You think this is *The Brady Bunch*? You show you love me when you can support me."'"

"You know *The Brady Bunch*?" I asked.

"Everyone in Korea knows *The Brady Bunch*." He broke out into song. "It's the story of a lovely lady."

"Yeah," I said, quickly cutting him off, "I haven't seen that show in years."

"Have you seen the movie?"

"The movie? Of *The Brady Bunch*?"

"No. *Letters to Juliet*," he said. "Have you seen it?"

"I have. I watched it before I came."

He nodded.

In the movie, a woman writes a letter to Juliet, but it gets lost and doesn't resurface until many years later. One of the newer secretaries insists that an answer still must be properly delivered, and then of course the two lovers, now old, find each other again after all these years.

"That is your Hollywood," he said. "Always the happy ending."

"I don't believe in that either," I said. "Life isn't that simple."

Hyun-ki appeared at the door, the camera jiggling in his hands. The two Koreans spoke together and then they filmed the *Brady Bunch* letter, our host holding it up in his hands as if he were reading it.

Then, almost as suddenly as they had appeared, the Koreans announced their departure. I followed them to the reception area, where they exuberantly thanked everyone for their time and walked toward the door, humming and nodding. Giovanna, her smile tight, ushered them out. *"Ciao,"* she said, then, *"Ciao,"* again, when they stalled at the entrance, bowing to each of us in turn. She was on her third *"Ciao"* when they finally squeezed out the door and everything became quiet again. Giovanna shot me a look and I fled back to my office.

An hour or so later, I was done. The endless letters were blurring my vision. I made my way to reception, where I found Giovanna by herself at the round table. She had a small pile of letters in front of her.

"You still answer letters?" I asked.

"Twenty or thirty letters a day, every day."

She has been doing this for more than two decades. I did some quick calculations in my head—that was at least three thousand letters a year, and maybe over a hundred thousand letters over the course of the time she'd been working here. I began to see my day's paltry efforts as a whisper in a hurricane, a pebble on a mountaintop.

"Arrivederci," I called at the door and Giovanna looked up from writing with a genuine smile, the first I'd seen from her all day.

17

"I will see you tomorrow?" she asked, laying her letter aside.

"You will," I answered. "You will."

———

The next morning, I headed to the office on my own. The Old City sits in a loop of the Adige River, and I made my way through the narrow streets. Church spires and red-tiled roofs rose above me until I passed through a gate in the medieval walls and a wide piazza opened before me. Off in the distance, the ancient Roman coliseum sat like a crumbling crown. I headed east onto the bridge, and on the other side, I dipped under a cement overpass and came along the Via Galileo, a long, straight boulevard that took me, at last, to the offices of the Club di Giulietta.

Giovanna stood behind the front counter. "Ah," she said, when the door wheezed open. *"Buon giorno."*

"Hi."

She tipped her head. "Your office is waiting for you."

I took that to mean I should get to work. I smiled at her and walked down the hallway to the little room at the back. I answered letters, uninterrupted, for most of the morning.

On the second day of answering letters, I began to see patterns in them. The vast majority were from young women, but there were outliers. One older woman wrote that she was not asking for advice for herself. She had three daughters, she said, two of them happily married but the oldest was alone. Could Juliet help?

"Every daughter, and every son too," I answered, "should wish to have a mother as thoughtful as you."

Only occasionally were there letters from men, and almost immediately, I could spot the difference in the tone and sentiment. Sergei from Russia wrote: "Women don't like me. I can't lead them to close relationships and then to sexual relations." Oh, Sergei. I'm pretty sure I see your problem. I wrote back to him that by writing to Juliet in the first place, he was showing a softer, more sensitive side of himself and that maybe he should work on showing that side to women.

"Dear Juliet," wrote a younger boy, "I'm so sorry that everybody puts his hand on your boob. It's really stupid. You are sweet and you make people believe in true love. Thank you."

And that was about as charming as a young man could be.

There were problems with translation too. A Chinese girl wrote of her English boyfriend and her struggles to communicate with him. She was fluent in English, but still the nuances were hard for her. "Speaking English," she wrote, "is like being underwater, and speaking Mandarin is like coming up for air."

Toward the end of the morning, Giovanna appeared at my door. She studied me silently.

Finally, she said, "Glenn, I am having some problems with this one." She laid a letter down in front of me and I saw with some pride that it came from Canada. The first line read: "I am married to a man who can be quite a doofus at times."

"This word," Giovanna said, jabbing at *doofus*. "I do not understand it."

"It's slang," I said. I grinned at Giovanna, but she remained impassive. "It's a sort of, well . . ." I stumbled on. "I can answer that one, if you like, and maybe you can take this one."

I shuffled through the pile and found my very first letter, the one from the woman whose husband had died, the one about Harry. Giovanna scanned it quickly. "Yes," she said, "I can answer this one." She disappeared down the corridor with the letter and I heard her whisper the word *doofus* to herself, committing it to her considerable English vocabulary.

I worked through the afternoon, feeling generally overwhelmed by the heartache in most of the letters. This was supposed to be fun, something I could tell my students about when I got back to Canada.

But there was more to it than that. I was looking for patterns in my own thinking. I was looking to learn from these letters. I was looking for some hint of what I should do about my own situation. I had to admit, so far, I didn't seem to be getting anywhere.

By four o'clock, I'd had enough. I packed up my things and headed down the hallway. Giovanna looked up from the table at the front. She'd been sitting, again by herself, answering letters.

"Ah," she said rising, "you are still here. Can you help me with something?"

"Um . . . okay."

She went behind the front counter. "There," she said, pointing at a cardboard box. "Could you carry that outside for me?"

The box was filled with letters like all the others. On the side, written in black felt pen, were the words SENZA INDIRIZZO. I wriggled my fingers under the base of the box to lift it. The damn thing probably weighed a hundred pounds. "Where do you want this?"

"In my car. Wait, I must find the keys," she said, rummaging through her purse.

I struggled across the office, trying not to spill the letters. Outside, Giovanna opened the passenger door of her car. "Here, in here."

I thumped the box down onto the seat. "What does *senza* mean?" I asked, straightening and stretching out my clenched fingers. "*Senza* something?"

"*Senza indirizzo*. It means there is no return address. We cannot answer these ones."

"But," I said, trailing her back into the office, "where are you taking them?"

"The inferno," she said.

"Hell? You're taking them to hell?"

Giovanna shook her head. "No, no. What is the word . . . incendiary?"

"An incinerator?"

"Yes, That's it. We do not throw them out with the rubbish. They are . . . too important."

"But surely there must be . . ."

Giovanna stared me down and I went silent for a moment. Then I remembered. "In *Romeo and Juliet*," I said, "there's a letter that is never delivered. It's the one thing that could have prevented the whole tragedy."

Her eyes softened. "Sit down," she said. "I will tell you something."

I sunk into a chair at the round table.

"It is sad," she began, "that all these people feel they cannot tell the person they love of their concerns. They write to Juliet instead."

"Juliet's not real," I said.

"No, she's not. But she is a symbol."

"I understand that."

"What did I tell you on the first day?"

"That I should be a fortune-teller?"

"Before that."

"You said that it is enough for people to write."

She nodded. "We are human. We all feel love. Maybe the senders feel they cannot send their message to the people who most need to hear it, but it's enough that someone, anyone, should hear their declarations."

"But they need an answer. Isn't there something we can do?"

"If there is no return address, we cannot write back. If there is, then we give them acknowledgment."

"But is acknowledgment enough?"

"For now, they are overwhelmed, you understand? All of them are feeling love and it is only for us to give them our ears."

"I guess so."

"It is an honorable thing that we do here."

I knew what she was trying to tell me, though the whole letter-answering thing felt like a bit of a grim slog. "Yes," I answered. I felt like I should add "ma'am," but I didn't.

"Now," she said, waving a hand at the pile of letters in front of her, "I have work to do. Yes?"

"Okay."

"Va bene." Giovanna pursed her lips and tipped her glasses to scrutinize another letter. I slipped toward the door.

"We will see you tomorrow?" she asked, looking up at me just before I left.

"Of course," I said. "I'll be here."

2

Teach me how I should forget to think

I taught Shakespeare to (mostly) compliant teenagers for more than twenty years. They had a let's-just-get-this-over-with attitude when we started, but almost always, within just a few lines, they were hooked—especially with the play *Romeo and Juliet*—and that's because I told them right at the beginning, even before the first fight scene, there were some very dirty jokes.

I wouldn't tell them what they were, though I would slow my voice at line 26, raise my eyebrows a little, and one or two of the students would catch on. I'd hear strangely chaste giggles—caught before they could get too loud—and watch the other grade tens students swivel, trying to understand what they had missed. After that, they were all sitting up straight, listening intently.

I used to tell my students that Shakespeare planted these hooks on purpose—just as I was now doing. In London in the late sixteenth century, everything south of the River Thames was questionable territory. The taverns were there, and the bearbaiting pits, and—don't make me say this, kids—women of the night. Prostitutes. Many of the students would look at me in horror. Funny, you'd expect teenagers to be more rebellious or at least coolly nonchalant, but my experience was never that. They were strict moralists, almost all of them.

The boys were the hardest to engage. But I had my ways. At the beginning of *Romeo and Juliet*, there's a street brawl between the Montagues and the Capulets. "Devin," I called out. Devin was a loud kid who sat midway back in the row nearest the door. In class discussions he often took over, debating like a politician, though he looked like Woody the cowboy from *Toy Story*.

"Devin," I said again, "come on up here."

Devin looked at me as if it were some sort of trick. His face was a sea of freckles, but he was at that stage of adolescence when he thought he was much more grown-up than he really was. He eyed me like a gunslinger. In a traditional classroom, as he well knew, the front of the class was the teacher's stage. The students were the audience, sitting passively at their desks. I grabbed a wooden yardstick from the chalk gutter under the blackboard. I hoisted it up and gave it a few swooshes through the air like a sword. "C'mon," I said again.

Devin approached warily. "Let's do the fight scene," I said, leveling the yardstick at him.

His eyes brightened. "Really?"

"Yeah, c'mon."

I handed him my yardstick while a few sedate cheers rose from the other boys in class. Then I hurled the insult that provokes the fight. "Do you bite your thumb at me, sir?"

"What?" Devin asked.

I picked up a ruler from my desk, considerably shorter than Devin's yardstick. "I said, do you bite your thumb at me, sir?"

Devin stood there, the yardstick hanging at his side.

"Say yes," I stage-whispered.

"Yes?"

"Then have at 'er." I rushed forward with a thrust and the students broke into cheers and laughter. We parried back and forth a few times, the wood of the rulers clicking and clacking. Then I called out to Sadia.

Sadia sat in the front row. She wore a hijab, a headscarf. Her family had immigrated to Canada when she was only a little girl. She was one of the brightest—and most unorthodox—students in the class.

"Sadia, you're the prince," I said. "Prince Escalus."

"The prince is a boy," someone called out.

"Says who?" I barked back, holding up my ruler to deflect a blow from Devin. "Prince Sadia, get up here and stop this fight. Quick!"

Sadia stood. She held her copy of *Romeo and Juliet* book in front of her with both hands and in a faltering voice said, "Halt."

Devin and I stopped.

"Um," said Sadia, searching for the right lines. "*Rebellious subjects,*" she said, "*Enemies to peace . . . throw your mistempered weapons to the ground.*"

"Mistempered," someone snickered.

Devin dropped the yardstick. It clattered to the floor.

"Good," I said. "Good." I glanced up at the clock. "That's about all the time we have today," I said.

"But what happens next?" asked Devin.

"Well, the bell's about to go," I said.

"Aw, c'mon, Mr. Dixon. Just give us a hint. What happens next?"

And that's when I knew that I had them.

———

I first learned about Verona and the letters to Juliet from the back of the *Romeo and Juliet* edition I used for years with my students. Like a lot of Shakespeare texts, this one had the difficult words and passages explained in the margins. It had illustrations of things like partisans (nasty-looking medieval weapons), rosemary (whose tiny blue flowers signify remembrance), and Cupid, the cherub, shooting his arrows of love. At the front of the book was a drawing of Shakespeare's Globe Theatre and at the back, a short selection of poems and essays about the star-crossed lovers. One of the excerpted essays was titled "A New Career for Juliet: Advice to the Lovelorn," from *Smithsonian* magazine in 1979.

That essay caught my attention. The article quoted a couple of sugary letters and I toyed, momentarily, with the idea of having my students write letters to Juliet. I never did, though. I thought there would be privacy issues, and I wasn't sure I wanted to deal with that. And now that I'd actually been to Verona, I didn't want to add to the secretaries' workload. I thought that sometime later, I'd just tell my students about the office there and the letters that pour in every year. In fact, I was looking forward to describing the real Verona to my students—the cobblestone squares and the medieval fortifications of the old town, the red-tiled roofs and the sunbaked bricks under a bright Italian sky. I thought they'd like that.

———

The sun was cantankerously hot, though it was barely ten o'clock in the morning. I thought I knew my way to the offices of the Club di Giulietta. I'd made it there the day before without any trouble, but today when I crossed the bridge, I zigged when I should have zagged, and found myself lost in the city cemetery.

I blame Napoléon. He decreed that all the cemeteries under his domain were to be built outside the city walls on account of the plague. This cemetery was massive. I stumbled through the tombstones, scampering beneath columns of cypress trees that offered patches of shade. The sun glared so sharply off the white-hot marble of the tombs that the names and dates were impossible to read. I kept moving east and eventually I came out on the other side. I hadn't gone very far down the road when I heard the *meep meep* of a car horn, a small car, a European car, sidling up behind me.

"Are you lost?" Giovanna reached over and opened the passenger door for me.

"No, I—"

"You are mistaken with your direction. Our office is over there."

"I know. I . . ." Runnels of sweat were trickling down my forehead. My shirt was plastered to my back and it wasn't anywhere near the hottest part of the day.

Giovanna looked at me hard. "I'll take you to the office," she said.

"Thanks." I clambered into her car.

From the back seat came a muffled giggle.

I turned and saw a young girl, maybe eleven or twelve. She balanced a wrapped present on her lap.

"I am taking my daughter to a birthday party. This is Margherita," Giovanna said, glancing up into the rearview mirror before inching the car out onto the road.

"Hi," I blurted. Margherita toyed with the bow on the present and allowed herself a shy smile.

"I must take something from the office," Giovanna continued, "but I will not stay. Anna will be there, though."

"Okay." I had no idea who Anna was.

When we pulled into the parking lot, the same blue bike from yesterday was leaning against the brick wall and the front doors were propped open. Margherita waited in the car, but I followed Giovanna in and down the hall to the office at the back. Across from it was another office, where a younger woman sat. Anna, I presumed. She was on her cell phone but she held up a hand. She said a few more words, then cupped her hand over the phone for a moment. "Hello," she said. "I must take this call. I'm sorry."

"Yes," said Giovanna, steering me into my own office. "You can meet Anna later. Now," she said, "you know what to do?"

"I think so," I said.

"I will return shortly. You will be here?"

"Yes. I'll be here." I saw the cardboard box of English letters leering at me. "I'll be here all day."

Giovanna frowned. I still don't think she knew what to make of me, and I wasn't quite sure what to make of her either.

"Ciao," she said, then whisked back down the hallway.

It was quiet after that.

I wiped my forehead with my sleeve and lifted a layer of letters from the box, fanning them out on the counter. They really were from all over the world—Brazil, Ukraine, Hong Kong, Argentina. And these were just the ones written in English.

"Dear Juliet," read the first one of the day, from Australia, "I'm in love with someone and he doesn't love me back. It rips my heart apart and I don't know how to move on. He's the first person I think of in the morning and the last person I think of at night. Please help me."

I wrote back some fluff about "this too shall pass." Easily said, but this girl was really suffering and I didn't think those words would help much. I twirled the pen between my fingers. I was trying to do what Giovanna had said—offer an empathetic ear—but I felt like it wasn't enough. For the last two days, I'd been offering clichés as answers, and every time I did, I felt like a fake. Wasn't there something more I could tell all these people?

I'd done some research on love before I'd come to Italy, and I turned my mind to it now. In the last few years, some really interesting studies have emerged on love, explaining how it slams into us, how it grabs ahold of us, and will not let us go. According to the research, love is hardwired into the reward center of our brains, says Dr. Helen Fisher, one of the leading experts in the field. Much of the research now focuses on evolutionary psychology, on the ways in which our brains have evolved over hundreds of thousands of years, and on the subtle behaviors that ensure our genes will be passed on to succeeding generations. Love is related to the powerful urge to mate, of course, but more exactly, it is the yearning for someone who will be around long enough to help raise a child. And that, as utilitarian as it may sound, is at the root of love. Love is, in that sense, our biological destiny.

This sort of love is fueled by dopamine. In the presence of the one we love, dopamine gushes into our caudate nucleus, exactly the same center in the brain that lights up in those addicted to crack or alcohol or gambling. Love, then, is an addiction—as anyone who has ever truly been in love can affirm. It takes us over, wholeheartedly, and makes us do some pretty foolish things. The letters I'd been reading were a testament to that, as was my own experience.

I'd fallen for women and literally waited for years for the relationship to evolve into what I really needed. It was all so stupid. It was such a waste. But enough with the remembering. I pushed my chair back from the desk. What to say to this heartbroken Aussie? She deserved something more than what my poor experience could tell her. In the end, I hunched over the letter and wrote: "I know what that's like. It hurts like hell, doesn't it?"

I heard Giovanna's footsteps coming down the hall. She hadn't really been gone long at all. She bustled into Anna's office and when I leaned out a little, I could see them. They were bent over a book on Anna's desk. Giovanna glanced up and caught me watching them. "Glenn," she called. "You have told me you know the Shakespeare."

"Um, yes. I know it."

"Can you help us?"

I pushed some letters aside and heaved myself up.

Anna's office was much nicer than mine. She sat behind a sturdy oak desk set on a royal-blue carpet. Everything was orderly and neat in contrast to the hurricane of papers scattered around my little cell. Anna peered up at me through green-framed glasses. She wore her hair in a stylish bob, and I guessed that she might be in her late twenties.

"Probably you will know this line," she said: "*Any man that can write may answer a letter.*"

"From *Romeo and Juliet?*"

"Yes!" Her eyes sparkled. Anna had a perky sort of earnestness and her voice was sonorous, reedy almost, like a clarinet. "Of course it is from *Romeo and Juliet.*"

"We have used this line in our e-mail," Giovanna explained, "but we are not certain we know exactly what it means." They both studied the book again and I could see now that it was the text of the play. One side was in English. The facing page was in Italian.

"Ah," I said, stepping closer. "That might be the scene where Capulet's servant is inviting people to the party, only he can't read the guest list."

Anna squinted down at the book. "Where is that?"

"Here, can I . . ."

The three of us searched the text. "Here's Benvolio," I said. "No, wait, it's later. It's Mercutio. It's the bit where he's making fun of his enemy, Tybalt. It's right before the big fight scene."

"Fight scene?" said Giovanna. She didn't look pleased.

"Here," I said. "Yes, Mercutio says it."

"Ah," said Anna. She penciled down the act and scene number.

"That line is in your e-mails?" I asked.

"It is," Anna said.

"You're answering letters by e-mail now?"

"Sure. At the House of Juliet. There are computers, and from there the people can send us an e-mail letter, instead of a real one." Anna shrugged. "We don't like it so much."

Giovanna pursed her lips in distaste.

"Probably I will say that writing a love e-mail is cheating," said Anna. "But it is the twenty-first century. We must allow it."

"We have many problems these days," Giovanna broke in. "At the house there are problems with chewing gum."

"Chewing gum?"

"On the walls," Giovanna said. "The people have attached their notes on the stone walls with chewing gum."

"Probably," reasoned Anna, "the chewing gum is good for thinking. They chew and chew and think what they will write."

"Yes, but it is disgusting," said Giovanna. "Now the city has made a new law and they have carabinieri in the courtyard. Policemen."

"The gum police," I said.

Anna stifled a smile.

"Now we have not so much gum at the House of Juliet," Giovanna said. "But we have another problem, have you seen?"

I had, in fact. I'd noticed it yesterday. On the walls under the archway leading into the courtyard were hundreds and hundreds of Band-Aids, small strips with short messages—like tweets on Twitter—felt-penned onto them.

"But what about the policemen?" I asked. "Can't they do something?"

"They cannot stop it. There are too many people. People always find a way." Giovanna stood up straight.

"It's better than gum, I guess," I said.

"Band-Aids are for flesh wounds," said Giovanna.

"Flesh wounds," I repeated.

"Yes," said Anna. "But in the case of our work, we treat wounds of the heart. It is not the same."

————

It was only our second day studying *Romeo and Juliet* when Sadia shuffled in her seat and said, "I don't know about this." We were still in act 1, scene 1, when the Montagues and the Capulets are first introduced. We'd not even seen Romeo yet.

I frowned at Sadia, wondering what was coming.

"Sir, how are we supposed to know this play is really about true love?" She tugged a bit at her hijab, pulling it a quarter inch down lower over her forehead. I'd noticed she did that when she was thinking.

There were gasps around the room.

"What are you getting at, Sadia?" I asked.

"They're young, right, Romeo and Juliet? Didn't you say Juliet was, like, thirteen?"

She has not seen the change of fourteen years, Juliet's nurse declares early on in the play. I'd told them that already. Juliet's age, in fact, was going to be a question on the quiz they'd get at the end of act 1.

"So, like, how do you know it's not just infatuation or something?"

A boy at the back of the class spoke up. "God, Sadia, because they die for each other, okay?"

"Any idiot can die," said Sadia. "And thanks for wrecking the ending."

"We already know the ending," I corrected. "It says so right in the prologue."

Sadia, stone-faced, glanced down at her book and flipped back a few pages.

"*A pair of star-crossed lovers take their life*," I read from the prologue. "It's right there—barely six lines into the whole play."

There were nods of agreement.

"They were so young," said Sadia, wistfully.

"How old was Romeo?" another student asked.

"It doesn't say in the text—but probably fifteen, sixteen, something like that," I answered.

"Like us, grade tens."

"Yes," I said pointedly. "Exactly like you."

———

The envelope had Winnie the Pooh on it. I withdrew the pink letter. "My name is Audrey and I am fourteen years old," it began. "I have a real tragedy. I lost my best friend because I thought I loved him. And now I've lost the courage to ever love again. Because if I try to love somebody, it just makes me hurt and I do not understand. Dear Juliet: Tell me why love hurts so much."

Yet another question, the same question I'd been asked over and over again. What was I to tell all these young girls? The truth? Yes, love hurts and there's probably a lot more in store for you. I couldn't say that, though. I tapped my pen to my lips. This girl was only fourteen— about the same age as Juliet. She deserved a genuine answer as much as anyone else. I was also sure that Giovanna would kick me out if I started to get snarky at people.

"Dear Audrey," I wrote back. "Love is as perennial as the grass." I stole that from *Desiderata*. It sounded good and I thought it was mostly true. There'd be other boys for her. There was probably another one already.

Done, I thought, reaching for another letter. "Dear Juliet," the next girl wrote, "please send me my Romeo. Send him to San Antonio, Texas."

"It is beyond my power," I wrote back, "to send someone to you, but if you truly want love, you need only be open to it and it will appear."

I sat back and reviewed my penmanship. I have messy boywriting. The words were okay, but I wasn't sure about the sentiment. It read a little bit like a fortune cookie, but it would have to do for now.

A few letters later I came to a rare one from a boy: "My teacher is making me write this letter and I think it's really stupid. But," he began tentatively, "there is this girl . . ." Then he plunged into a full and detailed confession, writing for almost two full pages in sloppy looping letters. At the end, I imagined him pausing and taking a deep breath before adding the final sentence. "So, seriously," he wrote. "Help me out here."

I knew what he meant.

For me, it's getting harder to dig down through time, to really remember what I was like when I was younger. It's hard to even imagine that I am the same person now as I was when I was fourteen. But I am. The same feelings echo through the archeology of my soul.

I suppose everyone has their proto–love story, an early love that sets the stage for all the rest. Tammy Brenner may not have been my first kiss, but hers was the first kiss I cared about. Tammy was cute and spunky, and I'd met her on the swim team when I was in grade eleven.

When the long summer nights came and school was done for the year, a few of us would sneak out of our houses and meet in the school yard. On one of those rare nights when the temperature was as warm as the day, four or five of us met in the shadows and walked up a hill into a grove of poplar trees. A languorous moon hung fat in the sky. Below us the world was etched in silver. Somehow, Tammy and I wound up sitting together, apart from the others, off in the trees. I was sixteen. She was a little bit younger.

Not much happened. Reality is often awkward and urgent, but memory smooths over the bumps and wrinkles. Tammy and I talked and laughed, and at some point, she kissed me. That moment remains with me, a star in the summer sky of my life. It never got better than that. Not only did it not get better, my love life got distinctly worse. There weren't a lot of triumphs in those early years. And even into my adult life, things have not really gone well in the ways of love.

Years and years later, out of the blue, my sister asked me, "Do you remember Tammy Brenner?"

"I think I remember her," I answered. Of course I did—she was pivotal in my early life.

"I just heard she died."

"What?"

"Breast cancer. She couldn't have been more than forty or so."

"Thirty-eight," I said, and I remembered the girl and that night long ago on a silver hill among a grove of poplar trees. My throat tightened and I turned away, pretending nothing was wrong.

———

I heard Giovanna's busy heels tapping up the hallway, and then a rustle of papers at my door.

"Hello?" I said.

She eyed me from the doorway.

"How was the birthday party?"

She shook her head and raised two fingers to her temple. "Very noisy. The children are very noisy. Do you need anything in here? It is going well?"

"Yes. But there are so many letters." I held my hands to my head in mock frustration.

She didn't say a word.

"And most of the senders," I barged on. "They're so young."

"Can I see?" Giovanna stepped into the room. I showed her my most recent answer, half-penned on the stationery in front of me. Yet another young girl asking for her Romeo. "You should go out," I wrote, "and do things, join clubs, try some sports, learn a musical instrument—find the things that you enjoy doing and perhaps you will find someone there who enjoys doing the same things, and wouldn't that be perfect?"

Giovanna's lips compressed.

"Not good?" I asked.

"No, no . . ." she said, handing the letter back to me. "It is a good idea, but . . . do you mind?" She sat down in the chair beside me. "You are not the psychiatrist," she began. "Maybe she is not looking for solutions."

"I know, but I'm trying to help. I'm trying to give her something practical that she can——"

"You are thinking she is a foolish young girl."

"She *is* a young girl." I looked at her letter. "Rachel. She's seventeen. From"—I turned the envelope over—"Birmingham."

"You are answering like a man."

That caught me off guard. "Pardon me?"

"They only want to tell their stories, to get their feelings out. Do you understand?"

I had no idea what she was talking about. "I think so," I said.

"*Va bene,*" she replied. And before I could ask her anything else, she stood, patted down her dress, and left.

————

My students bustled into class, chatting and full of hormones. We were barely into the new semester and some of them still got lost in the halls and arrived late and frazzled. Sadia arrived first. She found her seat at the front. She flipped her copy of *Romeo and Juliet* open, impatient for the rest of the class to settle in. Devin came in a minute or two late. "Sorry," he said, and headed for his desk near the windows, midway back. Outside, the sky hinted at snow. I waited as the students filed in and took their seats.

"All right," I began. "Where were we?"

"The prince came and stopped the fight," said Devin.

"Ah, right," I said. "Now we meet Romeo." I looked around the classroom, at the thirty teenagers rustling in their desks. "At the beginning of the play," I said, "Romeo is madly in love with a girl. But it's not Juliet."

A few of the students' heads popped up from their books, confused. Sadia's hand flew up.

"Yes, Sadia?"

"Who?" she demanded. "Who's he in love with now?"

"Well, I'm not sure I'd called this one 'love.'"

"But who?"

"Her name is Rosaline. And the thing is, she's not into him. At all."

Andy, near the back, was staring at me with particular attention. He was a big kid, stocky. I think he was on the rugby team.

Sadia cleared her throat. "So Romeo likes her, but she doesn't like him?"

"Right," I said. "And Romeo's cousin, Benvolio, is trying to help him out. They're best friends. So, what would you say to your best friend if he was in love with someone who didn't love him back?"

Andy's face flushed.

"Andy?"

"A friend?" he asked, looking around.

"Yes. A friend."

"I guess I'd tell him to try and . . . I don't know . . . forget about her."

I read from my textbook. "*O teach me how I should forget to think.*"

All heads bowed to their books. The clock ticked. It was so quiet, I could hear it. We had plenty of time to get through this first act. Maybe we would even make it to the balcony scene by the end of the week.

"What if," I said, "Romeo has absolutely no chance with this girl, this Rosaline? It says here that she has promised to live chaste. What do you think that means?"

"No sex," mouthed Devin, and titters rippled down the rows of desks.

"Yes, but more. It means she doesn't want to have a boyfriend, any boyfriend, right now."

"I think she's just saying that," Sadia said. "You know, to spare Romeo's feelings."

I smiled at Sadia. "I think you're right."

"She's letting him down easy, sir."

Andy looked uncomfortable at this revelation. He cast a sidelong glance at Allison, who sat over a couple of rows. Allison was studious and quiet, pretty, with long, almost jet-black hair. She was born in Hong Kong and had the slightest accent, but, like Sadia, she'd lived here most of her life.

"So she lets him down gently," I said, "but Romeo is pretty broken up about it. You can't help who you fall in love with, you know."

A few of the kids nodded knowingly. Andy shifted in his desk.

"Do you all really believe that?" I asked. "Is it true that we can't help who we fall in love with?"

Sadia considered her book again. "Maybe Romeo's just in love with being in love."

Andy's head shot up. He was looking at me almost helplessly.

"I think you're right again, Sadia. That's the question here. Does he really *love* Rosaline?"

"I guess not," Andy said, and a few heads swiveled to him.

"So what makes you say that, Andy?"

"Well, maybe she's just a pretty face. But that's not love. That's, like, attraction or something."

Everyone was turned around now. Andy stopped, well aware that he had become the focus of attention.

"Actually," I said, "Shakespeare has something to say about this too. Look at page 51." I waited as the pages rustled. "Lines 68 and 69."

Young men's love then lies
Not truly in their hearts, but in their eyes.

"Do you get it?" I asked. "It's a play on words—about lies. Young men are attracted to the visual, but maybe that love isn't real. It's a lie, not from the heart."

"That's so true," Sadia began, a touch of self-righteousness in her voice. "Most guys care only about what a girl looks like."

Devin grimaced. I could see that he was about to say something but thought better of it.

"Totally," Andy said. "If you're really in love, then that means you consider someone's personality too. It shouldn't matter what a person looks like."

Allison was looking at him now, and he stopped.

"But it *does* matter," said Devin. "A guy is not going to like some ugly girl."

"Devin!" barked Sadia.

"Hold on," I said. "We're getting a bit offtrack here. We're talking about Romeo and his supposed love for Rosaline, remember?"

One by one, the teenage attention spans angled back toward me.

"Romeo is head over heels in love," I said, "but it's unrequited love."

Andy nodded, and a few of the kids mouthed the word *unrequited*. For all its sadness, it is a beautiful word.

"So what's Romeo supposed to do?" I asked.

Sadia squinted. "You said Benvolio helps him. Can he make Romeo forget about this girl?"

"Maybe," I said.

"But how?" Andy pleaded. "How can you just forget? I mean, how can he forget about this girl?"

Everyone was focused now. They were waiting for my answer. Students are good at that. "There's only one way for him to forget," I said. "He has to meet someone else."

"Juliet," said Sadia. "He has to meet Juliet."

"Bingo."

———

They say that men fall in love more quickly than women. A pretty face is enough to set us off. The slight hint of a curve beneath a sweater. It doesn't take much. We're really quite shallow.

All of us, in fact—male or female, regardless of sexual orientation—

are attracted to a wide range of subtle cues in others. We're hard-wired that way. A strong, square jawline in a man is seen as attractive precisely because it indicates a healthy level of testosterone. A softer, rounder jawline in a female face marks a high level of estrogen. It's Mother Nature tricking us into choosing the one who is the most fertile.

And for both sexes, facial symmetry is a key physical attractor. Studies show that the most respected politicians—John F. Kennedy, for example—often have highly symmetrical faces, the left half being an almost exact mirror of the right. Many movie stars too exhibit symmetry. Asymmetry can be so subtle that we'd be hard-pressed to identify it—but our brains seem to unmercifully register minute variations.

The same goes for hair. A person's hair is a week-by-week, month-by-month calendar of their health, and it's on full display to everybody. The shiny, vibrant locks you see in shampoo commercials are signs to the viewer that this person is virile, that this is someone who will produce healthy babies.

Or at least that's the underpinning of evolutionary psychology.

We are inclined to fall in love with certain types too. We become enamored with particular features, what one researcher called love maps. I think my map was set when I was twenty or so, young enough to still be slurried in hormones and dumb enough to think it was something mystical.

After Tammy, I thought a girl named Mandy was the one. It helped that this Mandy was a willowy beauty. I'd been working as a lifeguard for a few months when she walked onto the pool deck for the first time. She had joined the diving team and, well, I think my heart stopped for a second. I was completely smitten. It was definitely love at first sight. She had cascading blond hair and the pool chlorine made it glisten like gold, like the halo on an angel. Or that's how I saw it anyway. Really, it was just root damage.

You know how sometimes you hear a new word and then all of a sudden you begin to hear it everywhere and you wonder how it was that you'd never come across it before? It was like that. The universe had somehow conspired for me to see this angel everywhere. At the pool, I asked around and I learned her name. Someone said they knew her cousin, and very shortly, someone was phoning the cousin and it was all arranged. Mandy would be brought to meet me at the pool for my next lifeguarding shift.

She trailed in behind her cousin. They walked into the pool area in their one-piece swimsuits, stepping lightly on the wet tiles of the deck to stand under my lifeguard chair. I was pretty sure I looked cool. The cousin called up to me, but I froze. Suddenly, faced with the goddess in my presence, I went silent. I didn't know what to do, so I jumped down and threw Mandy in the water. I'm serious. I just picked her up and tossed her in. She thought that was funny. What a ham. What a joker. But truthfully I did it because I was too astonished to say a damn thing to her.

So it started with a laugh and a splash, but it never went anywhere. I don't think I was ever comfortable talking to her and really, I was in love with a vision, anyway, not a person. My obsession with her lasted a year or two and plowed some very deep ruts into my topographical map of love. And that, I suppose, set me up for a whole string of relationship disasters.

———

I'd done my best with the answers, straining through another letter or two, when I heard Giovanna coming down the hall again. She'd been out front answering the phones with an efficient and abrupt, *"Pronto?"* But now she was bustling into Anna's office. Something was happening. I heard a shuffling and a quick conversation in Italian. Then they both appeared at my doorway.

"Toc, toc," said Anna, knocking on my doorframe. "I am going home for lunch now, but after, I must collect the letters from the House of Juliet. Do you want to accompany me?"

Behind Anna, Giovanna's taut smile told me I should say yes.

"Collect the letters?" I asked.

"From the postbox at Juliet's house," said Anna. "It's full again. We must empty it every three days." Anna looked at her watch. "Let's see each other there at four o'clock. Is it okay?"

"Sure."

"You know where to go?"

"Juliet's house. The mailbox in the courtyard."

"Exactly."

"Four o'clock."

An hour or so later, I walked back across the bridge and into the Old City. I thought I could get something quick to eat and then go a bit early to the courtyard. I hadn't seen the inside of Juliet's house yet and had enough time for a quick visit.

The courtyard was a throng of people snapping photographs in front of Juliet's statue. I glanced up at the balcony. It is a beautiful old feature, carved with two rows of tiny ornamental archways. I knew it wasn't a part of the original house, but it was still something ancient, and it cast a certain spell over the courtyard, just as it was intended to do.

I edged around the crowd and in through a door into the gift shop on the main floor of Juliet's house. A young woman sat behind a reception counter, but she hardly looked up from her book when I forked over my seven euros. She fluttered a hand in the direction I should go, up the stairs behind her. I clomped up a few of the wooden stairs and then stopped. Up just a few steps, on a tiny landing where the staircase turned ninety degrees, a full-size copy of the Juliet statue stared down at me. It was identical to the one outside, a bronze, life-size cast of Juliet. On this statue, though, the right breast was cracked like a broken eggshell, and the jagged triangular hole was big enough to put a hand through.

"*Questa è l'originale,*" the attendant said, looking up from her book.

"What?"

"This Juliet is the first," she continued in English. "The Juliet outside, she is only there since two months."

"That's a replacement statue out there?"

"Yes. You can understand why." I examined what was left of Juliet's right breast, scarred by a hundred thousand wishes for love.

"The Juliet outside," the young woman went on, "she is dark in color and we are worried she will never go gold, but she does." In two short months, the new statue's breast was already polished and shimmering from all the groping.

The young woman smiled and turned back to her book, and I thumped up the rest of the wooden steps to the first floor. Everything was clean, almost Spartan. No one had lived in this house for over a hundred years. And except for another much older woman sitting on a chair in the corner, a meager attempt at security, I was alone. Outside in the courtyard, the crowds still bustled and pushed but inside, my breathing was the only sound. The house bore architectural elements rescued or plundered from medieval palaces around the city; it looked like a stage set. I moved to a little side room, where the balcony jutted out, an alcove with Venetian arches. Should I step out onto it? It didn't seem right somehow to walk out there alone.

I smiled at the security woman in the chair and continued on past her, up another set of stairs, to a larger room on the second floor. A massive fireplace took up one wall, with two high-backed chairs set in front of it. Over the fireplace was a copy of the Cappello coat of arms—the same emblem of the bowler hat that was set in the bricks above the courtyard. The rest of the room was empty, with planked floors and huge shuttered windows. This was meant to be the ballroom where Romeo and Juliet first met.

In another room, in glass cases, were costumes from the Franco

Zeffirelli film of *Romeo and Juliet*. Juliet's dress looked heavy: thick, brocaded wool sweeping down to the floor. Romeo had a tunic of blue-and-gold vertical stripes and a billowy white shirt underneath it. I remembered the exact scenes in which he wore it. A few of the Montague boys had snuck Romeo into the Capulet party, hoping to distract him with other girls, hoping he'd get over the heartbreak of Rosaline. And it worked. He saw Juliet across the dance floor and was instantly smitten. *"Did my heart love till now?"* he declared. *"For I ne'er saw true beauty till this night."*

––––––

"Do you think it was love at first sight?" I asked the class.

"I don't know," said Devin. "That seems kind of dubious."

"You're dubious." Sadia whirled around in her seat, facing Devin head-on.

"C'mon," he said. "It's just a story."

"It *is* just a story," I jumped in. "But if Shakespeare was anything, he was a genius at capturing how people really are. He was all about writing something real, you know, about the human condition."

"Dubious," Devin repeated under his breath. Sadia grumbled at him, making a low menacing sound in her throat.

"Romeo sees Juliet across the room," I went on. "He's interested for sure. She's dancing and he says, *'I'll watch her place of stand.'* In other words, he's going to watch where she goes to stand after the dance." I paused. "I've been there," I said.

Sadia raised her eyebrows. "Been where?"

"To Verona. I've been in the room where Romeo first saw Juliet."

A few more heads popped up, wondering if I was laying a trap. Teachers do that sometimes and these students knew it.

"You've been to Verona?" Sadia asked.

"To Juliet's house, yes. It's a real place."

"But this is a story. It isn't real."

"I know. But there was a Capulet family and there's this old house that belonged to them. On the second floor, they have a big hall. Supposedly, that's where Romeo and Juliet met."

Devin glanced at the clock.

I decided to move on. "Anyway," I said, "Romeo ambles over to where Juliet is standing and he brushes his fingers against Juliet's hand ever so lightly, as if it's an accident. That way he can stop and say sorry to her. It's just an excuse to talk to her."

"Smooth," Devin mouthed.

"Exactly," I said. "Boys, pay attention. This is pretty good."

Andy grinned at me. Even Marc, a rough kid sitting at the back, cocked his head.

"Take a look at line 95. Andy, why don't you read that?"

Andy's grin disappeared.

"C'mon," I said, "there's nothing difficult in this part."

Andy cleared his throat. "*If I profane with my unworthy hand.*"

"Unworthiest."

". . . *unworthiest hand this holy shrine, the gentle sin is this: my lips, two blushing pilgrims, ready stand to smooth that rough touch with a tender kiss.*"

"So what's he talking about?"

"I have no idea," Andy said.

"Well," I explained, "it's religious imagery. Romeo is saying to Juliet, 'I am like a pilgrim come to see a holy shrine, and you're that shrine.'"

"In this room you went to," Sadia said, "was there a shrine?"

"No, no, it's just a figure of speech."

"You mean like Romeo is putting her on a pedestal, like she's some sort of goddess?"

"Exactly. Romeo's often over the top like that. Juliet, on the other hand, is more pragmatic."

Sadia nodded.

I scanned the room. "Allison, how about you read Juliet's lines?"

45

Allison didn't say no, but her voice rose a little in pitch, tight and nervous. "*Good pilgrim, you do wrong your hand too much.*"

"Now, Andy," I said, "you read Romeo's lines."

I let them stumble through the dialogue until the stage directions say they kiss. Andy pulled to a stop, a red blush creeping up his thick neck.

"They've hooked up," said Devin.

"Yep. They are about to kiss. They've been testing each other. Like in a game of chess or something. Look carefully," I said. "Romeo says four lines, then Juliet says four lines. Look how it rhymes. And look how it goes on for exactly twelve lines like that, back and forth."

Sadia studied the text.

"Then they each say a single concluding line. That makes fourteen. Do you get it?"

"It's a sonnet," said Sadia.

"It *is* a sonnet," I said, "buried right in the middle of the scene."

"Are you allowed to do that?" said Sadia.

"And it's the very first words they say to each other."

"That's kind of cool," said Sadia.

"Do you see what I mean now, when I say that Shakespeare is the master?"

Devin nodded. Andy was still glowing over his reading with Allison, keenly imagining the stage directions where they were about to kiss. Tough guy Marc at the back had his eyes glued on the text, still counting the lines.

"The whole point," I went on, "is that they each see the other is intelligent, that the other has a sense of humor. They are enjoying the give-and-take. It's not just physical attraction. They really like each other.

Sadia scrunched her lips together. "It's still pretty fast."

"This whole play takes place in five days," I said. "From beginning to end, it's five days in their lives."

46

Sadia started to grumble. "Five days? That's kind of crazy."

"Maybe you shouldn't take that literally. Sometimes you have to play with time to tell a good story."

"And then Romeo kisses her," Andy piped up, eager, I think, to get back to the story.

"Yes, and what does Juliet say to that?"

"*You kiss by the book*," Allison read. "What does that mean?"

"Ha," I said. "Scholars have been arguing over that line for centuries. It could mean that Romeo kisses perfectly. You know—like a textbook example of a kiss. But . . ." I paused. "Do you think you could learn to kiss from reading a book?"

"No," Andy blurted. Then he quieted and sunk down behind his desk.

"Exactly," I said. "There's no instruction manual for love, no matter what anybody says. You can't learn about love from a book. *That* would be crazy."

———

It was nearing four o'clock. I didn't want to miss Anna, so I stepped back into the daylight, into the crowds, and spotted her standing by the archway that led to the street. Two younger women were with her, all of them scanning the crowd for me. Beside them, set into the stone wall, was the red letter box. *"Scusi,"* I called, elbowing my way through the tourists.

"You are here," Anna said. "Good." She held up a large brass key. "Soňa, Veronica, this is Glenn."

"Hi," I said.

Soňa clutched a tote bag in both hands. Her blond hair was tied back in a ponytail, though the tips were tinted an almost copper color. She wore glasses with canary-yellow frames. "You're the Canadian?" she asked.

"That's me," I said.

Behind her, Veronica grinned. She looked young—a teenager—and even Soňa was probably only in her early twenties. Veronica looked Italian, with long dark ringlets of hair. Soňa not so much. Were they really secretaries? Were people so young allowed to answer the letters, or were they merely collecting them?

"Allora," said Anna, "we open it now." She clicked the key into the padlock and lifted it from its eye hook, then swung open the tiny door, handing the padlock over to Veronica.

Soňa pulled the tote bag open and held it under the letter box while the letters spilled out. Behind us, a few tourists were snapping photos.

"Chiudi la porta," said Anna.

"Yes, boss," snapped Soňa, swinging the door closed. Veronica clicked the padlock back into place.

"To the other office," Anna said.

"There's another office?"

"Yes. But it is difficult to find," Anna admitted. "You must walk until you are lost, and then you must go a little farther."

The four of us walked up the Corso Porta Borsari, a wide street that started with an ancient Roman gate and ended at a medieval church. The lane opened into a triangular courtyard. A bright orange Vespa scooter hovered on its kickstand there, and from a window above came the clank of cutlery and the smell of frying onions.

Anna unlocked a door tucked into one of the corners; inside, a flight of marble stairs led up to an open foyer. We crossed over to a glassed-in room and waited for Anna to unlock that one too. She flicked a switch, and fluorescent lights hissed into being.

"This office," Anna explained, "was a goldsmith's shop three or four hundred years ago. It's very old."

Soňa heaved the tote bag onto a table in the middle of the room and turned it upside down, shaking out all the letters, her bracelets rattling.

"Now we sort them," said Anna.

Veronica plucked one from the top. "English," she said, creating an English pile. Anna found an Italian one and started another pile. She picked up a third but passed it over to Soňa. "Russian," Soňa said.

Four pairs of hands flitted through the letters, like a lightning game of rummy, and in fifteen minutes or so, we had more than a hundred of them sorted into stacks by language. A whole world of heartbreak.

"Shall we answer a few?" asked Anna.

"Sure," I said. "Let's do this thing."

———

It's time now to fess up. I was in Verona for a reason. There was somebody in my life, but it wasn't going according to plan. In fact, it was kind of messed up.

Let's call her Claire.

I'd met Claire when we were both still in university, almost twenty years ago. We were doing our master's degrees—different faculties, mind you—but within the first few moments of talking to her, I felt not just like I'd met someone but like I'd discovered someone. Someone, finally, who was a lot like me. It was a revelation. I'd been in love before—or so I thought—but this time it seemed different. This one seemed right. This was how it was supposed to be. I guess you could say that I fell in love with her right from the start. She was pretty and smart, but it was more than that. She seemed to "get" me, just as I seemed to "get" her.

She had a boyfriend when I first met her. I knew that. I also knew that it wasn't going well with the guy. He didn't like the idea of her being in grad school. He thought it was a waste of time. Once, she told me, he flew off the handle when she used what he considered big words—words with more than two syllables, words like

49

accumulate. Claire launched into an imitation of him: "What the hell kinda ten-dollar word is that?" She stopped and shrugged.

"That's preposterous," I said. "Who gets angry over vocabulary?"

"Completely egregious," she said.

"Incongruous, vexatious," I added.

"It's proprietorial," she continued, "and highly solipsistic."

I couldn't top that, so I stopped.

Claire fixed me with her jade-green eyes. "I guess you can't choose who you fall in love with," she said.

"No," I said, "I guess you can't."

At Juliet's house, on the very top floor, the ceiling is lined with painted stars. Hundreds of six-pointed stars fret the ceiling between the ancient wooden beams, orderly rows alternating in white and mustard-yellow. I knew what they symbolized: Romeo and Juliet were star-crossed. They were meant to be together.

Shakespeare references stars throughout the play. Our fate is written in these stars; all our loves, all our foibles, all our missed opportunities tracing unalterable paths through the heavens and, whether or not we like it, this is our destiny.

I know now that that's not true. That's all horseshit.

Star-crossed

On my way to Italy, I stopped in London. In the formidable British Library, among a collection that holds such treasures as the Magna Carta and Gallileo's drawings of the moon, there is a very old manuscript of *Romeo and Juliet*. The so-called second quarto is nearly perfect. It's the text from which most other copies derive, and it was printed in 1599, only three or four years after Shakespeare wrote the play. In fact, it's likely that Shakespeare sanctioned this printing, and it's almost certain that it was printed from his original handwritten manuscript.

I'd spent months applying for permission to see the quarto. I had to become a member of the British Library. I needed a special security clearance, which meant explaining exactly why it was so important that I see it in the flesh, so to speak.

And finally, though I'd done everything properly, my application was denied. That seemed to be the end of that, until a few days later I got an e-mail from a member of the Rare Books and Special Collections Group. Tanya Kirk was her name. She said she'd looked at my application and was intrigued. Could I send her some more information about my intentions? I did. I told her all about the Club di Giulietta. I told her that I'd taught *Romeo and Juliet* to high school students for twenty years. I quoted lines from the play, and I must have sounded pretty earnest because within just a few hours, she replied. "Right, then. We will make a special exception. You must present yourself at the security desk at five p.m. on the tenth of August. We are just off King's Cross station and you must not be late."

So there I was on the appointed day, straight off the plane, trying to feign alertness but addled by jet lag, scruffy with travel. When I got to the British Library, the security guards at the front desk balked. They scanned their computer and insisted I had no appointment.

"No," I said, "Tanya Kirk has made an exception for me. I'm supposed to meet her here at five."

They eyed me suspiciously. Phone calls were made. There was much glaring at the computer screen, until Tanya Kirk herself appeared behind me. She was younger than I'd imagined. She wore hipster glasses and a necklace with big blue baubles. "Don't mind the guards," she whispered. "Just follow me."

Tanya led me down a flight of stairs into the basement of the British Library and stopped in front of an unmarked metal door. She pulled a lanyard from her pocket and pressed the security fob against a wall-mounted sensor. The door buzzed open and then we were heading down a corridor. It could have been a custodial hallway under any busy office building. "Not very glamorous, is it?" she said.

She buzzed us through another door and we entered a large room with a hive of cubicles. It looked like a call center. I had no idea what all these people were doing. Tanya showed me into a small conference room off to the side with just a bare Formica table and a whiteboard on the wall. "Wait here a moment. I'll be right back with the quarto."

When she returned, she carried a small cardboard box that opened like an envelope. She set up two gray Styrofoam platforms on the table. They were angled so that a book would sit open in their wings. And then she took out the Shakespeare manuscript. I'd imagined some oak-paneled room. I'd imagined white gloves and a silver platter. But now the manuscript lay before me, nothing like I'd imagined.

It was so small, not much bigger than my two palms. I'd spent months working to attain permission to see this—the second quarto of *Romeo and Juliet*—and now, here it was.

"How did you know," Tanya asked, "to ask for the second quarto?"

"The first is called 'the bad quarto,'" I said. "It's two years older than this one, but it's missing almost half the lines of the play."

"That's correct," she said.

It's generally agreed that the bad quarto was put together by one of the actors in Shakespeare's company. That actor's lines are all there, but for the other characters in the play, the lines are only sketched in or just skipped over. The gist of the story is present, but so much is missing or just plain wrong that the bad quarto is rarely ever consulted.

"The second quarto is the complete play," I said and Tanya nodded. She turned to the manuscript and opened it carefully. The pages were in almost perfect condition.

"You can see," she said, flipping to the end, "that someone has written in a date just after the last lines: 1621. It may have been the original owner."

I looked down at the print. Was she suggesting this could be Shakespeare's handwriting or—no, he was dead by then—but maybe that of someone who had known him? Maybe. My eyes swept back to the lines before the date. There they were. Lines that would ring out across the centuries:

A glooming peace this morning with it brings;
The sun, for sorrow, will not show his head.

For never was a story of more woe
Than this of Juliet and her Romeo.

I think I shivered involuntarily.

"Are you quite all right?"

"It's amazing." The text had the word *woe* spelled *wo*. Other than that, it was identical to the text I'd spent so many years teaching.

"Later," said Tanya, "this quarto was in the collection of King George the Third." She turned back a few pages. In the margins, here and there, were asterisks and penned-in notes. Someone had made a careful study of the text. "We can't know for certain," she said, "but some of these markings may be the king's."

"King George?"

"The Third," she finished. "He was the mad king."

"Right."

"When he died," she said, "this quarto was at Buckingham House, and the next king, George the Fourth, wanted the house expanded into a full palace."

"Buckingham Palace."

"Correct," she said. "So he had all the collections cleared out—like in an estate sale—and that's when this quarto arrived at the British Library. That was in 1812."

"Wow."

Her fingers hovered over the pages.

"Aren't you supposed to be wearing white gloves?" I asked.

"No," she said. "We don't do that anymore. With gloves, we've found that the pages are sometimes torn by accident or the manuscript can be dropped. We can't chance that. Skin is much more sensitive and much more responsive to the frailty of the paper."

She turned back a few more pages to Juliet's soliloquy in the vault. A dark smudge, like a water stain, covered half the page. "In World War II, the library was hit by a German bomb," she said. "There was some damage, mostly from the firefighters trying to put out the fires. I don't think this stain is from that, though. This one is probably older."

"King George reading it in the bath?"

"Perhaps." She smiled. "He did enjoy his baths."

"Can I see the prologue?"

"Of course." She flipped back to the elegant title page—*The most excellent and lamentable tragedy of Romeo and Juliet*, and on the next page was the famous prologue. There was no list of characters. In fact, this ancient quarto had no markings at all to show acts or scenes. Each scene ran into the next. *Two households, both alike in dignity, in fair Verona, where we lay our scene.* The font was beautiful. Some of the *s*'s looked like *f*'s, and here and there the spelling was different, but the text was complete.

"Can I see their first meeting?"

"Yes, just a moment." Tanya turned a few pages forward. There was the Queen Mab speech.

"Just past that," I said. "When they're on their way to the party at the Capulets'."

She skipped ahead a few more pages but went too far.

But soft, what light through yonder window breaks?
It is the east, and Juliet is the sun.

"Oh my God," I said. "That's the balcony scene."

Tanya looked down at the text. "So it is."

"Wait, can I read some of that?"

"Of course," she said.

"What's that?" In the margin was a tiny, finely drawn hand,

bunched into a fist, with the index finger pointing toward the printed text, almost like a graphic from the Monty Python show.

"That's called a *manicle*—from the Latin *maniculum*, 'little hand.' You find them sometimes, added to old manuscripts."

"Do you think King George could have drawn that?"

"It's entirely likely, yes."

I looked at the pointing finger, drawn by a king, maybe. It alighted on the lines *Two of the Fairest stars in all the heaven, having some business, do entreat her eyes to twinkle in their spheres till they return.*

"Stars," I murmured.

"I beg your pardon?"

"Oh," I said, waving my hand. "It's nothing."

———

If you go to Juliet's house in the middle of the night—and I'm not saying I did—you can't sneak in. It's locked up tight. An iron gate blocks the archway, but you can stand there, your fists on the bars, and gape in at the old house. It's quite magical. The courtyard is empty of tourists, shrouded in purple shadows, with a single spotlight shining up across the famous balcony. Now, I'm not saying that I had too much wine to drink. I'm not saying that at all. I'm just saying that I went for a bit of a wander, at night, under the stars, through the narrow medieval lanes of the Old City.

Ancient streetlamps cast dappling lights over the rushing black water of the river. Pigeons cooed in the roof beams, and wineglasses clinked in the outdoor cafés. I shuffled aimlessly, tramping down cobblestone lanes, until I suddenly emerged onto one of the brighter pedestrian streets, one I recognized—the street that led down to the piazza surrounding the Roman coliseum.

The opera was just getting out. People were streaming through the old Roman arches and into the piazza. It was after midnight, but children ran about, whooping and laughing. A few touts, knowing this, had toys for sale. The best one was a helicopter you could fling high into the air from a rubber-band launcher. These minichoppers floated down on whirling propellers, with little LED lights—purple and green—blinking as they descended. All the adults smoked. The burning ends of cigarettes bobbed in the dark like stars on the ocean. I wandered through the crowd, mostly couples, arm in arm in their pressed suits and evening dresses. And it made me feel alone. It made me remember why I had come. It made me think about Claire again.

———

Very shortly after I finished university, I decided to go traveling. I wanted to see the world and I'd set my heart on Bali, exotic, far-off Bali. To my great surprise, when I mentioned my plan to Claire, she asked if she could come along.

"Of course," I said, trying to hide my excitement. "That would be great."

At the airport, though, as she trundled up to the check-in counter with her suitcases, I could tell something was wrong. What I didn't know was that Claire was using this trip as closure. She'd broken up with her boyfriend—the one who didn't like large words—and in a bid to make it stick, she had arranged to flee the country, with me, only she didn't tell me about that little detail.

When we landed at the Denpasar airport, a mind-numbing seventeen hours later, we squeezed into a tiny bus that took us up to a place called Ubud. It was supposed to be a tropical paradise. Emerald-green rice paddies terraced up the hillsides. An ancient temple stood at the end of our road, a thousand years old, with demons and Hindu gods carved into the crumbling stone walls. Spider monkeys swung from the trees, and in the evening, we could hear gamelan music, chiming and drumming, drifting up from the temple complex. It would have been magical except that Claire did almost nothing but cry for the first few days—cataclysmic sobs—and there wasn't a damn thing I could do to help her.

She'd sunk into an emotional squalor. She had loved that boyfriend, even though she knew he wasn't right for her. I think now that he was the one who'd set her own personal love maps. In a way, I think she never really got over him. I tried to be unbiased about it, and I wish I could say that I became her knight in shining armor, riding in to save the day. But it wasn't that way at all. The world, for me, is not a romantic comedy. Claire just needed a friend, and I was, apparently, the one she had chosen.

Then it got worse. She got sick. Really sick. We phoned for a doctor and he huddled into our little hut without a stitch of English. He wanted to jab her with a needle though we weren't sure what was in it. We weren't even certain that the needle was sterile. We chased him out and she just lay on a cot, crumpled, for the next week, counting the hours until our return flight. I sat outside in a little garden, not far from the room, bringing her water when she called out for it, the magic of Bali forgotten and out of reach all around us.

We limped home after that. She'd lost a lot of weight and was inexplicably angry with me. Maybe she needed to be angry at someone. I too wanted to howl at the universe: *Wait a minute. Wait. This is not how it is supposed to go.*

But fate was not listening.

———

I spent a few late afternoons in Verona, just wandering and thinking. On a side street, not far from the river, I stumbled across the Korean Broadcasting System again. They were shooting more film footage by the old fortifications they call "Romeo's house." Of course, just like Juliet's balcony, this wasn't actually Romeo's house. A powerful family by the name of Montecchi did live somewhere in the vicinity of Verona seven hundred years ago. All the influential families holed up in fortresses in the fourteenth century—it was a dangerous time in Verona—but there's no evidence at all that this particular house belonged to the Montecchis or that they'd had a son named Romeo. Still, the imposing dwelling with its unbreachable walls is representative of the times. It was the kind of place an important family would have owned.

The Koreans were on the street outside the house. Hyun-ki, the handler/cameraman, was down on his knees on the cobblestones, crouching over his camera's viewfinder. Our host, whose name I couldn't remember, stood—bestriding the camera—and on cue, he sauntered away from it so that in the shot his hiking boots would appear first and then, as he walked away, he would recede, shrinking like Alice in Wonderland with the fortress walls rising above him. I stood in the shadows and watched them film this take a couple of times, each time changing something slightly—the camera angle, the speed of the host's walk.

On the third take, the host spotted me. He waved merrily, and Hyun-ki turned too with a wide grin on his face.

"Hello, Canada," said Hyun-ki.

The host strode forward, beaming as if we were old friends reunited after decades. "You have come to see Romeo's house?"

"Yes. I have. I'm sorry, but I can't remember your name."

"I am Ahn Sung-jin. In Korean 'Ahn' is the last name."

"Okay, Sung-jin."

"You call me Jin. Like your English 'Jim.'" He pointed at the door. "We cannot enter. We have tried to knock. Do you have a way in?"

I'm not sure what superpowers they thought I possessed. Just because they'd seen me at the Club di Giulietta did not mean I had a key to the city. Frankly, they probably had more access to the tourist sites than I did. "No," I said. "I've got no way in either."

The house had crenelated walls and a small square tower; in effect, it was a little castle. Quite unlike the other tourist attractions of Verona, this house was owned now by a private family who refused to have anything to do with all the hoopla and speculation over Romeo and Juliet. The family spent a lot of money on restorations and I assumed they lived quite comfortably in their fortress, the heavy oak door closed securely against writers and lovers and cameramen from Korea.

Near the door, they'd at least allowed a historical plaque:

TUT I HAVE LOST MYSELF; I AM NOT HERE,
THIS IS NOT ROMEO, HE'S SOME OTHER WHERE.

"Interesting," I said.

"What is this meaning?" Jin asked, his face lined with bewilderment.

"It's a bit tongue-in-cheek, I think."

"Tongue-in-cheek?"

"An inside joke—saying that this is not actually Romeo's house so that people won't bother them, so people will go away."

"But what is 'Tut'?" he asked, tilting his head.

"An exclamation, like 'oh,' though maybe a bit impatient or disapproving."

"But I am so sorry, I am not understanding this."

"It's Romeo who says that line," I said. "He's means he's not feeling like himself these days."

"Because he is in love?"

"Yes, exactly."

"Ah," the host nodded. He explained to Hyun-ki in Korean, and there was more nodding of heads, humming, and pondering.

"You in love?" Hyun-ki asked turning to face me.

"What?" The personal question came out of nowhere.

"You come here because you are love story?" Hyun-ki pressed. Jin grinned behind him.

"Well, I, you know . . . I . . ."

"You always travel alone?"

"Um, yes, sometimes."

"You not married?"

"No, I'm . . . well, there is someone, back home." I paused. "But no, I'm not married." I could see from his facial expression that this was the wrong answer. "Are *you* married?" I managed.

Jin stepped in. "I have been married for ten years already. Hyun-ki for fifteen."

They both had children. They both had houses and jobs and families and, though they didn't mean it that way, I began to feel I should slink off with my tail between my legs. Before I could, Hyun-ki muttered something in Korean and they excused themselves with much bowing. "We must go now. We are seeing the opera tonight."

"The opera?"

"You have seen the opera, at the arena?"

"Oh, right," I said. "In the old Roman coliseum. I haven't been yet."

"Tut," said Jin, shaking his head.

"So, what's playing tonight?"

"Tonight it is *Aida*, but tomorrow night is *Romeo and Juliet*."

That stopped me. "*Romeo and Juliet* is an opera?"

"Yes."

"I didn't know there was such a thing." There was that lush Tchaikovsky overture. And of course, *West Side Story* was loosely based on *Romeo and Juliet*. At least I knew that much.

"Tonight, it is full up."

"Sold-out?"

"Yes, yes, but tomorrow night, tickets are most available. We are going. You will go too?"

"Well, I hadn't really—"

"Tut," he said again.

"Okay, yes. You're right. I'll get a ticket."

———

The following night, I did go to *Romeo and Juliet*, the opera. The setting is spectacular. The Arena di Verona is not just any concert hall; it's a massive Roman coliseum built in the year 30 CE. It sits in the middle of a wide piazza, and it's large enough to seat fifteen thousand people. Now though, instead of gladiatorial fights, it hosts operas—lavish spectacles that draw tourists from across the continent of Europe.

Before the show, I had some pretty decent spaghetti carbonara at a café on the edge of the piazza. I took my time, waiting for the long summer twilight to dwindle. The shows start only after it's dark, but when I saw the crowds starting to form, I finished my meal and dug out my ticket. I went in through a pink limestone arch and up a set of marble steps worn by two thousand years of foot traffic. My seat, my three square feet of rock bench, was near the top and, fortunately, the man at the front desk of my hotel had given me a thin foam cushion to put down over the cold marble, which was good, because it was to be a very long performance.

Everyone in the audience was given a small candle upon entry, and when the candles were lit, the arena became a constellation of stars. A full orchestra fronted the mighty stage, and the opera began with two hundred or more singers marching out to sing the opening chorus. I assume it was the prologue; it was all in Italian and it was magnificent.

Then, not more than ten minutes into the story, a vehicle drove onto the stage. It had a propeller at the front and huge hydraulic wings that opened into a satanic umbrella. It looked like the car from *Chitty Chitty Bang Bang*. Wait a minute, I thought. I don't remember this anywhere in Shakespeare, and certainly not in *Romeo and Juliet*.

A woman clambered out of the car, dressed head to toe in red leather, brandishing a whip. She cracked her way through the male singers—Romeo and Benvolio and Mercutio—who all bowed down before her. What the hell? Who was this character supposed to be? Rosaline? The Devil? Love Incarnate?

She leaped back into her Batmobile and a terrific pyrotechnic column of flame *whomped* from the vehicle's back end. The crowd cheered as she drove off. I checked my program. Was I at the right play? After that, the Prince was wheeled onstage in a contraption that looked like a glazed flowerpot—only it was two stories high. Juliet, like a magician, in what I think was the balcony scene, released two doves from her draping sleeves. The poor birds fluttered and flopped onto the stage, where they pecked at the floorboards for the rest of the act as the singers swirled around them. Several rows below me, I caught sight of the Korean Broadcasting team. They turned at one point and waved up at me, gleeful smiles on their faces. They were having the time of their lives.

The night wore on with tumbles of musical scales and incomprehensible stage settings. I followed as best I could, trying to fit the Shakespeare tragedy I knew so well with what was unfolding on the stage below me. I assumed one singer was Tybalt, but then the woman in red leather appeared again, prancing about him, whipping him and others at random. Another guy appeared on a two-story-high saltshaker. That had to be Friar Lawrence. Was this the wedding scene? I had no idea.

In the end, I was completely lost. Juliet had stabbed herself with the dagger; then she rose up—a couple of times—to sing a few more arias. Romeo, who had long since poisoned himself, kept lifting his head to throw in the harmony. Finally, the Prince showed up again on his flowerpot to call an end to the shenanigans.

It was well after midnight when we were let out into the piazza. The Koreans were waving me over to them.

"You like?" Hyun-ki asked. He was vibrating with excitement.

"I don't know what to think."

"I like very much." He touched his heart.

Jin bowed to me. "We are leaving tomorrow," he said. "You are staying?"

"Yes. I'm still answering letters."

"And you are learning something about love?" He hummed solemnly.

"Yes, I'm trying."

"I wish you good luck and safe travels."

"Thanks, Jin. Same to you." He bowed again. And then I bowed to Hyun-ki and he bowed back and then they bowed to each other, and this could've gone on for a while had I not interrupted. "Really," I said, "It's late. I should probably get going."

They bowed a few more times and then they were gone.

I wandered across the piazza, past a statue commemorating some long-forgotten battle. The night was calm, the old cobblestones still warm from the day's heat, and I kept on walking, past the turn for my hotel. What was I doing here? What was I hoping to accomplish?

I guess I'd thought that all these letters would tell me something real about love. Something I could learn. But I had my own problems, and maybe, I thought, maybe the first step should be writing my own letter to Juliet.

———

I'd had a couple of late nights out in Verona, and I was finding it harder and harder to drag myself down to the offices di Giulietta, or at least to make it there much before nine in the morning.

I'd also forgotten what it was like to write with a pen for hours, the cramping in the meaty heel of my hand, having to stop to shake it out, every so often, like an injured bird. And no matter how many letters I answered, more and more kept avalanching across my desk.

One letter came from a girl in England. She was doing her sixth form—which is something like grade twelve—and she quoted almost the entirety of the prologue from *Romeo and Juliet*. "I want to be in the theater," she wrote. "I know everything about the play. I have studied it all my life."

You should have been at the opera last night, I thought. Maybe you could have explained it to me.

"I don't really believe in true love," she went on. "I think, anyway, I will have to sacrifice a husband for a career. Having said that, the idea of being in love is very attractive. I don't want to be lonely. Should I let love be a priority, or should I continue to let my head rule over my heart?"

I paused before answering. "Your dreams are important," I wrote. "They are what make you you. The right person will understand this. I wish you luck. Maybe one day you will perform Shakespeare onstage. Maybe one day you will direct the play you love so much."

I read the answer over. Not bad. I didn't want to give this girl false hope, but I didn't want to spoil her dreams either. I was trying to be a grown-up. Giovanna would like that. She'd told me from the first day to put my answers into the envelopes but not to seal them. I imagined she and the other secretaries checked my answers. Maybe, maybe not. All I knew for sure was that someone, sometime later, would type the return address on the envelope and off the letter would go, back into the real world, eventually arriving at a faraway mailbox, giving the original writer a little electric jolt of pleasure and surprise and maybe, just maybe, an answer to their questions.

———

I responded to one last letter, then stood for a midmorning stretch. On the wall behind my chair, a poster of Gustav Klimt's *The Kiss* gave the office its only color. Beside the poster, taped to the whitewashed wall, was a small square of yellow paper. I leaned in to read it. *"Ogni pensiero, ogni sentimento ed ogni azione . . ."*

"Only" something? "Only sentimental," maybe? I gave up and sat back down. I wished I'd made more of an effort to learn Italian before I'd arrived. I had borrowed an Italian grammar book from a friend of mine, Desiree. She was fluent in Italian and she'd lived in Italy for almost eight years. I'd barely cracked her book open, though. There never seemed to be enough time.

Just as I pulled another letter toward me, Giovanna's daughter, Margherita, appeared at the door. She held up a plastic desktop clock, then plunked it down onto my desk with a frozen grin like that of a synchronized swimmer.

"What's this for?" I asked.

"Per sapere l'ora," she murmured, then reversed herself out through the door.

Across the hall, Anna was craning her neck to see what was going on. "What did she say?" I called over.

"She said, 'The clock is for telling time.'"

Was Giovanna trying to tell me something? I knew I was getting a little lackadaisical with my departures and arrivals, but it didn't seem particularly Italian to be worried about punctuality. Besides, it wasn't like I was getting paid. I glared at the clock, but it wasn't giving me any answers.

———

After the disaster in Bali, it didn't take long before there was another boyfriend and then, a few years later, another one after that. In the end they weren't good to her—or so I thought—but they were square-jawed and handsome and I knew I couldn't compete. I was stymied. Like an insect trapped in amber, I'd been fossilized as her friend. I tried a few times to reiterate how I felt, but she would explain, patiently, as if she were discussing an idea from our university days. "I love you too. But I'm not *in* love with you. There's a difference."

I wasn't sure about that. I wasn't sure about that at all.

Still, it was a friendship worth holding on to. She and I would talk for hours, having conversations like I'd never had before. We'd discuss Foucault and Darwin and Adam Smith. She could speak with authority on the theory of conspicuous consumption and quote whole passages of *Alice in Wonderland*, all of "Jabberwocky," for instance, playing with the words, as happy as a child.

The average human has a vocabulary of about sixty thousand words. Some of us, like Claire, have more. The funny thing is that 98 percent of all conversations—about anything—use only about four thousand of the most common words. So what are all the rest for? One theory has it that the rest are there for courtship, that they are displays of intelligence, just as facial symmetry is a display of health. I'm not sure I quite believe that. Words are not peacock tails. Words mark meaning, in deeper and deeper levels of subtlety. They are critical to our understanding of one another, to the expressing of our deepest thoughts and feelings, and recognizing those in others. Physical attraction is one thing but really seeing into the soul of another person—that should be more important, shouldn't it?

A pathway runs along the riverbank where I live. You can walk across a footbridge and off into a forest of Douglas fir trees. Claire and I walked there dozens of times, maybe hundreds of times over the years. She always had cold hands. Her fingertips would go white and then purple. Even on the brightest spring days, her fingers lost their color. She'd hold them up for me to see, shaking her head, surprised at their hue. On the far side of the river, train tracks run along a ridge. Long trains thumped through, carrying wheat and canola to the Pacific markets of China and Japan and India. Claire always waved to the conductors. They leaned out of their tiny windows above the roaring engines to make sure the tracks were clear ahead. She raised a hand with fingertips the color of amethyst and the conductors waved back at her. Once, after a long train had passed, she turned to me, glowing. "You're my best friend," she said, and I didn't know what to say in return. So I said nothing at all.

––––––

What is most useful in all the research on love? What is the most important thing to know? Well, probably this: Love is not just one thing. Love, by most accounts, has at least three distinct aspects. This is sometimes called the triangular theory of love and, for true love to exist, you need all three sides of the triangle: passion, intimacy, and commitment. And that requires some explaining.

Passion, in this case, is defined as lust or sexual desire. It's the tangible, the touchable—the kissing and hugging and, yes, the sex act. It's often the catalyst that gets the other aspects going. Or not. I don't know. Maybe intimacy and commitment can develop in other ways, but what we do know is that passion alone is not love. How many have fallen on the sword of that misconception? Romeo was attracted to Rosaline, there's no doubt about that, but he lusted for her. He didn't truly love her.

That brings us to intimacy, the second essential for true love. Intimacy here means trust and not just physical closeness. Implicit in the idea of intimacy is the sharing of your deepest self—your secrets, your fears, your dreams—with this other person, and that this intimacy is reciprocated.

The third aspect of the triangle is commitment. This is the conscious decision, freely made, to settle down with one particular person and only that person. It's the choice of monogamy, if only for a time. And how long that will last . . . well, that's up to you.

––––––

The clock read ten when Anna appeared in the doorway of my office. She held a sheet of paper in her hand. "Can you do me a favor?"

"Sure. What is it?"

She slid the paper onto my desk. "We are planning a city tour of Verona," she explained. "It is one of our ideas."

"Okay."

"We need new ideas for raising funds. We receive ten thousand letters a year, but the city pays only a set amount for the postage. It is not enough." Anna met my eyes. "It is a big problem, so now, probably, we need to find other possibilities to make money."

"So, a city tour?"

"Yes." She pushed her glasses up the bridge of her nose. "I want to know if the English is correct before I put it on the Web page."

"I'd be happy to look it over."

"Grazie mille," she said, "And don't worry about the Italian parts." She paused. "You don't speak Italian, do you?"

"No. I'm trying to learn some. I brought a grammar book. A friend lent it to me but I haven't really . . ." It sounded more pathetic with each phrase I uttered, so I stopped.

Anna stared at me. *"Va bene."*

"What is that? Everyone says that here."

"It has a thousand meanings, but probably it means something like 'okay.'"

I nodded.

"You say it now."

"Va bene?"

She kept a poker face for a moment; then her whole face lit up. "Bravo," she said. "That is a good try."

She bustled out the door and I went back to work.

Half an hour later, just as I'd finished the corrections, Anna appeared again, carrying a tray. "Coffee?" she offered. I picked up a tiny espresso cup from the tray. It was no bigger than an eggshell. I pinched its delicate handle and brought it to my lips. The espresso was as thick as melted chocolate, earthy and rich. *"Grazie mille,"* I sputtered.

Anna tipped her head graciously. She eyed the tour plans I'd been working on and I saw from her frown that she wasn't pleased with the number of pen-stroked corrections I'd made. I couldn't help it. I'd been an English teacher for a very long time.

"Va bene," I said, holding up the paper. "It sounds like a great tour."

Her eyes squinted through her emerald-green glasses as she studied my corrections.

"I like your glasses," I said.

"Green is my favorite color. It is my favorite since kindergarten." She touched the corner of her frames. "That is when I was first married."

"Pardon?"

"You know how children are. There was a boy I liked, and we played that we were getting married. We had the whole ceremony, and I remember that my dress was green. So green has always been my favorite color."

"And now?"

"What do you mean 'now'?"

"Are you married?"

"I just told you I am married."

"No, but really married. Or do you have a boyfriend?" I suddenly realized maybe I'd crossed a line. "I'm sorry, is that okay to ask?"

"I have very high expectations," she explained. Her forehead furrowed, but there was mirth in her eyes.

"Right," I said.

"He must be better than my first, and probably that will not be easy."

———

We know now quite a bit about what's going on in the brain when we're in love. Passion, for example, in the triangular theory of love, is all about testosterone. That's the chemical surge of sexual desire in both women and men.

Feeling close to someone, sharing your secrets, sets a whole different array of neurochemicals into motion. There's dopamine, the neurochemical at play in the reward centers of the caudate nucleus. But there's also norepinephrine and serotonin, the latter a neurotransmitter well known in the field of antidepressants. These neurotransmitters give us the giddy, happy feeling we have when we're truly growing close to someone. They give us the cozy pleasant lull we feel when we're having an intimate conversation over wine and candlelight.

As for long-term attachment, that's our brains producing oxytocin, a bonding hormone. This is the same neurohormone that makes goslings imprint on the mother goose. It's the same hormone that gushes around in pregnant women, bonding them to the baby about to be born. Oxytocin is a strange and powerful compound that we're only now starting to fully understand, and there's no doubt that it's flushing through our systems when we are in the presence of those with whom we've chosen to spend our lives.

These are the chemical moons that push and pull at the tides of love. These are the biological stars that bend us to our fates.

————

Just before one o'clock, Anna came in to collect the espresso cup. She was going to wash up, then head home for lunch.

"Anna," I said, "what does this mean?"

She looked at the yellow patch of paper tacked onto the wall. "'*Ogni pensiero, ogni sentimento ed ogni azione . . .*'" she read. "This means 'Every thought, every emotion, and every action . . .'" She read the next line silently. "Then, yes, these things it says are based on fear

71

or on love. *Amore* is love. You know this word, I think." She jabbed at the word on the paper.

"*Amore,*" I said.

She continued reading from the yellow paper. "*'Maestri sono coloro che scelgono l'amore.' Maestro*—do you know *maestro?*"

"Master?"

"No, it means 'teacher.' This line says that teachers are the ones who choose only love." Anna paused. "You are a teacher, are you not?"

"Yes," I said. "I am."

————

My students always seemed to know when the balcony scene was coming.

Sadia had been talking about it for days before we actually got to it, and at the appointed hour, she sailed into the classroom with a knowing smile. She pulled her hijab down over her forehead and opened her book, not even looking up as the others made their way to their seats. Even Devin arrived on time, which was unusual. He slipped into his seat without a word. A reverent silence hung over the classroom.

"*But soft,*" I began, "*what light through yonder window breaks? It is the east, and Juliet is the sun.*

"So," I said, "who is the sun?"

Andy squinted up at me, trying to work it out.

"It is the east and Juliet is the sun. Anybody?"

"Er, Juliet?" offered Devin.

"Yes. Now, why do you think Romeo is saying this?"

"Because he likes her?" Andy said. Poor Andy. He wore his rugby jacket every day in class. He was a fullback, broad across the shoulders but so new to his brawn that he shuffled and slouched uncomfortably most of the time. I could see that he was doing his best.

"Sure," I said. "Because he likes her."

Andy beamed.

"Okay, so—listen." I read on:

Arise, fair sun, and kill the envious moon,
Who is already sick and pale with grief,
That thou her maid art far more fair than she.

I glanced up from my book. Everybody had their heads buried in the text, even Devin. They hated when I interrupted, but I really wanted them to understand this. "Who is the moon?" I asked.

Sadia rose a couple of inches from her seat. "Rosaline," she announced. "Rosaline is the moon."

"Yes," I said. "The sun outshines the moon. Romeo has found someone who outshines Rosaline."

"In your face, Rosaline!" said Devin.

I kept reading:

Her eyes in heaven
Would, through the airy region stream so bright
That birds would sing and think it were not night.

"Yeah," said Devin. "That's good."

"You bet it's good," I said. "This is the greatest love scene of all time."

"But," said Sadia, "isn't he being kind of creepy, sneaking into her backyard and watching her through the window?"

"Balcony," Devin corrected. "She's come out on the balcony."

"Actually, if you look, you'll see that Shakespeare never says 'balcony.'"

"It just says 'enter above,'" said Devin. He gaped up at me. "Where's the balcony?"

"Well," I said, "in Verona, they do have a balcony at Juliet's house."

"You just said there wasn't one," said Devin.

"I said that Shakespeare doesn't mention one in the play. Now, though, it's become so much a part of our popular culture that in Verona, at Juliet's house, they added a balcony on the second floor."

"Why would they do that?" Devin asked.

"I don't know, but it's kind of beautiful."

"But it's fake," said Devin. "It's not in the play."

"Sometimes," I said, "imagination is as important as reality."

"People need stories," said Andy. "Even if they're not real."

"Yes," I said. "They do."

———

Everything I've told you about Claire happened long ago in the first few years that I knew her, just after we'd been at university together.

And then, after only a few years, she suddenly disappeared. She'd taken a position on the other side of the country and, in a way, that made things easier for me. I loved spending time with her, but I hated it when she opted for someone else, someone strikingly handsome. "It's like a scene from *Clockwork Orange*," I once told her. "I feel like I'm chained in place, eyelids propped open with toothpicks, forced to watch something I don't want to see."

"I'm sorry," she said, and I knew she meant it. She insisted again that you can't help who you fall in love with, but her approach to men did seem strange. Claire was brilliant. She was controlled and poised, and she often said that she wanted to live her life impeccably. Yet her relationships seemed a little impetuous to me. She could be as giddy as a schoolgirl, and I found that hard to understand. Until, of course, I realized that I was probably no different. There was nothing reasoned about my love for Claire—it was an instinctual and inextricable pull.

After she moved, we e-mailed and texted for a while, permitting ourselves all the artificial communications of the twenty-first century, but it was never the same. And in time, I didn't hear from her anymore—though I never stopped thinking about her. She was gone two years, then three, then four, and then I stopped counting. I settled into a life alone. No one else appeared to take her place and, frankly, I didn't give a damn. I was tired of being a complete idiot. I was done with love.

———

"Okay, where were we?"

The class hadn't quieted yet. The bell had rung but the students were still arranging their books and papers. I heard the heat duct kick in. At the front of the class, in the first row, Sadia pursed her lips and glared at her text but avoided eye contact. Several desks behind her, Andy snuck a glance at Allison. Devin, nearer the back, was surreptitiously stealing a last glance at his cell phone, so I stared him down until he pushed it into the black hole of his backpack.

"All right, everybody. Act 2, scene 2, line 55, do you have it?" Their heads tucked down to the text. "Juliet is talking to herself, and she's clearly a little put out that Romeo was eavesdropping on her. Listen: *What man art thou that thus bescreen'd in night so stumblest on my counsel?*"

Andy smiled and thrust up his hand, though I hadn't asked a question.

"Yes? Andy?"

"She's saying, 'What are you doing here? Why are you sneaking around in the dark?'" Andy leaned back and folded his arms across his chest, quite pleased with himself.

"That's what she's saying, all right."

Andy beamed.

"Then Romeo says, *With love's light wings did I o'er-perch these walls; for stony limits cannot hold love out.*"

"Nice," said Andy. He'd lifted his pen, about to copy that down.

"It's drivel, Andy. It's utter rubbish," I said.

Andy gaped at me as if I'd just defied gravity. "But it's Shakespeare."

"No, it's Romeo. And he's put himself and Juliet in a dangerous position by being there. Tybalt would kill him in a second. That's what Juliet is saying."

"So she's warning him."

"Yes."

"And Romeo is being kind of a jackass," said Devin.

"Devin," I cautioned, "don't push it."

Sadia put up her hand. "Isn't it supposed to be the girls who are the romantics and the boys who are the—"

"Jackasses?" Devin finished.

"Shakespeare doesn't stick to clichés," I said. "That's what's great about him but, Devin, seeing as you are perfect for Romeo today, you can read his lines."

"Oh, Mr. Dixon. C'mon."

"Sadia, you read Juliet."

Sadia coughed theatrically. For some ungodly reason, when she recited lines, she did so in a mock Scottish accent.

Dost thou love me? I know thou wilt say 'Ay,'
And I will take thy word: yet if thou swear'st,
Thou mayst prove false.

Devin looked up at me for the signal to read.

"*Lady*," he began, "*by yonder blessed moon I swear that tips with silver all these fruit-tree tops—*"

"She cuts him off here," I interrupted. "Sadia, go ahead."

Sadia *ahem*-ed again.

O, swear not by the moon, the inconstant moon,
That monthly changes in her circled orb,
Lest that thy love prove likewise variable.

She'd drawled out *moon* like an extra from *Bonnydoon*. "Isn't the moon Rosaline?"

"Could be," I said. "Or maybe here, it's just the moon. Do you understand it, though? Romeo tries to swear by the moon and she says no, the moon is always changing. Your love for me must be more consistent than that."

Sadia grinned. Devin didn't look happy. "*What shall I swear by?*" he went on, in a non-Scottish accent.

"*Do not swear at all,*" said our Braveheart Juliet. I held up my hand to stop her.

"That's good," I said. "Most directors have Romeo climbing up a tree or vines or something to get up to the balcony at this point."

Devin grimaced at me. "There is no balcony."

"I said it's not in the stage directions. They are both madly in love with each other, so most directors figure that you need to get them kissing here."

"Oh, Mr. Dixon." Sadia's cheeks blushed red.

"Now read on a bit, where Juliet delivers some real poetry, something from the heart."

Sadia read:

My bounty is as boundless as the sea,
My love as deep; the more I give to thee,
The more I have, for both are infinite.

"Can you hear the difference between her lines and Romeo's?"

Sadia sighed. "Romeo's just making up flowery stuff. Juliet's lines are . . . I don't know . . . more real."

Andy copied the lines into his notebook. Allison watched him do it. She was, it seemed to me, looking at him a little differently now.

———

The afternoons were sweltering in Verona. By two o'clock, the sun baked the streets and the shadows were short tiny circles around us. Anna and I walked to a little place where we could grab a slice of pizza, and we ate as we walked, heading toward the new office on the Vicolo Santa Cecilia.

A hot blue sky rolled above us as we cut through the University of Verona and over the Ponte Nuovo—the New Bridge—which has been there since 1334. Anna talked about her university days. She'd studied economics and marketing. She obviously had a head for it.

"When I finished the university," she said, "I traveled, like you. I went with Gloria—she's at the club sometimes, probably you have seen her?"

I wasn't sure who that was.

"All the time I was traveling," she went on, "I was thinking about my home in Verona."

"And?"

"You think Shakespeare's play is not true, but there is more to the story. Many people here believe it truly happened."

"I guess everyone can see a bit of themselves in Romeo and Juliet."

Anna stopped, midway on the bridge. The Adige River flowed beneath us, gurgling down from the Alps. "There are at least two Italian versions," she said, "more than a hundred years older than your Shakespeare."

"He's not really 'my Shakespeare.'"

"Glenn," she said, "why did you come here?"

"Because I thought it would be . . . interesting."

She stared me down. "Probably that is not all."

I took two deep breaths. "Well," I said. "I have a . . . a situation." I glanced out over the river. "It's a long story."

"We have some time," she said.

"I think maybe I should write a letter to Juliet."

"You? You will write to her? About what?"

"There is this woman. She's my best friend, but I—"

Anna's phone started beeping. She reached into her purse, holding up a finger to pause me. *"Pronto?"* she said.

I heard a buzzing voice on the other side, and Anna spoke back. She held her finger up to me again, then said, *"Ciao,"* into the phone three times before clicking it off.

"Are you hot?" she asked.

"What?"

"You like gelato? I know a really good place."

"Um, sure."

"The others are meeting there now. We can go before working?"

"Absolutely."

The Gelateria Savoia is one of the oldest gelato shops in Verona, maybe one of the oldest in the world. When Anna and I arrived, Soňa, Veronica, and another woman I'd not seen before were waiting for us out front. Inside the Gelateria Savoia, a crystal chandelier hung high above the counter. Soňa pointed it out to me. "There are two in the world," she said. "The other one is in the Hermitage, in Saint Petersburg."

I don't know if I even looked at it. I was too distracted by the metal pans of gelato behind the counter, rainbows of color, all shiny as silk. They wobbled a bit when our server punched into them with her scooping spoon. "Oh man," I said.

"*Fragola* is strawberry," Soňa explained. "*Cocco*, that's coconut."

"What's this one?" My breath was frosting the glass.

"Mango."

"I'll have that."

Soňa ordered for me. And before she scooped up the gelato, the barista squirted something into the bottom of the waffle cone.

"That's *cioccolato fondente*," said Soňa.

"We enjoy chocolate," said Anna, "in the bottom of our cones. It is really nice."

This was, without doubt, the best ice cream I'd ever tasted. I once heard the comedian John Pinette do a skit on gelato. "It's not 'Wow, that's good,'" he said. "It's 'Wow, I'm going to sell my house and everything I own just so I can move here and eat this every day until I die.'"

It was that good.

After, we strolled to the new office, cones in hand. Soňa dribbled a bit of gelato onto her shirt and shook her head at herself. On her T-shirt was a print of an owl.

"Nice graphic," I said.

Soňa dabbed at her shirt with a napkin. "The owl is for my initials. *So* and *Va. Sova* means 'owl' in Czech."

Anna turned to her. "So, you are an owl?"

"An owl is a messenger," said Soňa, "and I am answering the letters of Juliet. Like a messenger."

"Owls are messengers in many of the North American First Nations stories," I said.

"And in *Harry Potter*," chimed Veronica.

"In children's stories," I said, "owls are wise animals."

"Allora," said Anna, "then you have the wrong animal, Soňa."

Soňa stabbed her ice-cream cone at Anna. The two had a real Laurel-and-Hardy thing going on.

I thought I'd change the subject. "How long have you been here, Soňa?"

"Two months."

"Two months too long, Mrs. Owl," Anna said.

Soňa ignored her, though I could tell she liked the repartee.

"Get any really good letters lately?" I asked.

"Some are funny," said Soňa. "One letter asked: 'How many cats does it take to replace a boyfriend?'"

"What did you answer?"

"Five—and a hamster."

"Are you serious? Did you write that?"

"No. But that's what I wanted to write."

When we finally arrived at the new office, we sat around the wooden table in the middle of the room. We worked diligently for a while, until Soňa gave an audible intake of breath and we all turned to her.

"Look at these," Soňa said. She had two letters in front of her, side by side. She touched first one, then the other.

"Someone wrote twice?" I asked.

"No, no . . . look." She pushed them toward me.

Both letters were from Minneapolis, written by best friends, Emily and Marissa. They must have made a pact to write their letters to Juliet together. I'm not sure they read each other's letters, though, because if they had, they'd have been very surprised. Marissa was un-married. She was lonely. All her friends were married (and obviously that included Emily). Some of them had children already. It was so unfair. What had she done wrong?

Emily, on the other hand, had been married for six years. Her husband had been deployed to Iraq. He'd come back unharmed and, in fact, he hadn't changed much after his tour of duty. But she had. Her father had died while he was gone. She'd been seven months pregnant when he left, and she'd had to deal with a new baby all by herself. When her husband returned, in a shower of stars and stripes, she found she'd completely lost her libido. He wanted to make love all the time and she just wanted to be left alone. She felt terrible about it. He'd served his country. Was it too much to expect to come back to a loving wife? So she went on playing the part. And now that their daughter was born, she was trapped and uncertain and desperately unhappy.

I looked up from the letters. Soňa was watching me.

"Wow."

"What do you think?" she asked.

"They're both unhappy. It's as if they want to switch lives."

Veronica said something in Italian.

"What does that mean?" I asked.

Anna stepped in. "It is a saying: 'No one knows what part of the shoe pinches—if not the person who is wearing it.'"

"That's good," I said. "We have a saying: You can't know someone until you walk a mile in their shoes."

"It is the same," said Veronica.

"Even best friends," I went on, tapping at the letters. "They don't know what's in the other's heart."

Veronica leaned forward, "But we know," she said. "When we read the letters. They tell us."

"It's true," said Anna.

We grew quiet. Answering these letters was a solemn duty. We were the keepers of secrets. Giovanna had been right about that. The people who wrote entrusted us—or entrusted Juliet, anyway—with their deepest feelings, feelings they had to hide from the rest of the world, but feelings, all the same, that they needed to share.

———

Soňa was staying in a tiny apartment near the university and had to meet her flatmate. Veronica had to catch a bus back home from a bus stop on the Corso Cavour, and they'd both left already. My hotel was south of the Old City walls, but I stayed awhile longer to close up with Anna. At the door, as she was clicking the key into the lock, she looked hard at me. "You didn't finish your story," she said.

"What story?"

"About your letter. That probably you should write a letter to Juliet."

"Yeah, I should."

"*Allora*, what will it say?"

I shook my head.

"Come on. Tell me."

"Okay," I said. "Here it is." I started from the beginning and told her the whole sad story. It all made sense—up until the point where everything changed.

Claire, you see, had come back.

4

So smile the heavens

The days dwindled in Verona. I had to go back home in September to teach, and so, on one of my last mornings, before heading into the offices of the Club di Giulietta, I made my way through the cobblestone streets to see another of the city's landmarks—the place they call Juliet's Tomb.

South of the medieval walls, a busy street leads to the train station. Halfway down, an unremarkable lane veers between two high walls and opens up again into the grounds of a crumbling Franciscan monastery. At the entrance, surrounded by brambles and vines, a bust of Shakespeare sits in a niche. Beside it, bolted onto the stones, is another bronze plaque. A GRAVE? it reads. OH NO, A LANTERN. FOR HERE LIES JULIET AND HER BEAUTY MAKES THIS VAULT A FEASTING PRESENCE, FULL OF LIGHT.

The monastery of San Francesco al Corso was bombed during

World War II though an underground vault just past the medieval cloisters remained untouched. I walked across what was left of the gardens. An old wishing well stood in the middle of a grassy court-yard, and past that, a set of damp stone steps led to a cavern. No one else was around. I clunked down the steps. At the bottom, in an arched recess that looked almost Moorish, a candle flickered. I hunched under another archway and into the crypt itself.

A sarcophagus lay in the middle of the floor. This was, suppos-edly, Juliet's grave. Shakespeare's text portrays a family vault, but in this one, there was only a single stone sarcophagus, open at the top and empty inside. The stone was unadorned, and a deep crack ran down its side. Legend has it that Lord Byron chiseled off a piece of the sarcophagus to give to his daughter. Napoléon's second wife had several stone fragments made into earrings. Apparently, the very first letters to Juliet appeared here, when the postmaster of Verona had no clue where else to deliver them. A groundskeeper at the monastery was the first to collect the letters and answer them, and so, whether or not Juliet was real, this place was at least the spiritual home of Juliet's letters.

In my bag, I carried a notebook. The pages were dog-eared, filled with quotes and conversations, maps, and recommendations regard-ing my trip so far. I tore out a blank page and looked across at the old grave.

"Dear Juliet," I began. "It's been a long journey . . ."

The words flowed easily. I knew what to say. I'd known Claire for almost twenty years. The time had come to stop with all the ques-tions. The time had come for answers.

Once I'd finished, I gave the paper a crooked fold and tucked it into an old envelope. When I looked up, a group of schoolchil-dren were staring at me. They'd halted at the entrance, unsure if they should disturb me. I waved at them and stood, packing up my writing gear. I had to get to the office but later, I'd drop my letter in the bright red mailbox at the Casa di Giulietta, and that would be that. I'd be done with Verona.

———

This was not my first time in Italy. Just when I'd almost gotten her out of my head, Claire moved back. She'd been gone for six years and then, quite out of the blue, her job out east had vaporized and she'd been offered a new one back in the city in which I lived. It was abrupt and unexpected, and she was frazzled by it all.

When she first reappeared, it felt like only a month or two had passed. It was as if time itself was irrelevant for us. And when, in her new position, she was invited to a conference in Europe, I suggested that she should go see Florence. It wasn't far from where her conference was being held, and it seemed a shame to go all that way and not see Tuscany.

"Maybe I could meet you there," I ventured.

"Really?" she said.

I hadn't exactly thought this through, but I barged on. "It's just an idea," I said. "It's kind of crazy—but maybe . . ." I paused. "Just crazy enough that I should do it."

She chuckled at that. "You should," she said. "You should come."

It was winter when we arrived, and the crowds were nonexistent. It felt like we had Florence all to ourselves. A dark rain spattered the streets, but when the sun edged out from behind the clouds, the buildings were lit by a dramatic chiaroscuro light like a painting by Caravaggio. In the Academia, we rounded a corner and saw before us Michelangelo's *David*, his marble hand towering over our heads, his noble face lit by the heavens. It was so striking that Claire grabbed me by the arm and insisted that we go back and come around the corner again, just so we could experience again the sheer awe of seeing it for the first time.

Florence shone and Claire was entranced. Italy is like that. It casts a spell like no other place on earth. One cold but bright afternoon, Claire was going back to a shop by the Ponte Vecchio where she'd seen some shoes of Florentine leather that she wanted to buy. We stood across from the Duomo, the exquisite domed cathedral, and I was showing her the doors on the baptistery. They are fitted with panels of cast bronze by the sculptor Lorenzo Ghiberti and over the years the doors have come to be known as the Gates of Paradise. "Okay," she said, "let me go get those shoes and I'll meet you back here at three o'clock."

"Here? At the Gates of Paradise?"

"Sure," she said. "I'll meet you at the Gates of Paradise." She laughed and her voice chimed like earrings dropped into an empty wine goblet. She was beautiful when she was happy. Her jade-green eyes sparkled. She trundled off, but at three she was nowhere to be seen. I waited and was just starting to get worried when she showed up half an hour late, in a bit of a mood, and the bronze bas-reliefs—framed by angels—were all but ignored behind us.

Still, for the next year or two, Claire would tell that story at dinner parties. "I'll meet you," she said, shaking her head in delight, "at the Gates of Paradise."

Only she never did.

We were friends and, let me be honest here, there was no sex. Nothing had changed on that trip, and I found myself right back where I'd begun years before. Obviously this was not going to be a traditional relationship, but I began to think that there really were all sorts of relationships in the world and, if this was how it was going to be, then *c'est la vie*. I guess I'd deal with it.

But everyone yearns for a little magic. Everyone wants the Gates of Paradise to open for them, and when I wrote my letter to Juliet, it was one last knock on the door. It was one last attempt at a happy ending.

When I left Juliet's vault, I headed straight for the Club di Giulietta, and when I strode in through the door, I thought I'd made pretty good time. It was just after ten, and an old man stood by the front desk. He wore a canary-yellow tie and a navy-blue vest and he was reading the newspaper, *La Repubblica*. He refused to look up at me.

"Ah," I floundered, "is Giovanna here?"

He stood straight, proud, his yellow tie arrowing down his chest like a swath of moonlight on a dark lake. He clamped his lips shut and waved an impatient hand, which I took to mean, "She's in the back, you foreign monkey."

"Scusi," I said, scurrying by him. I could feel his eyes jabbing into my back as I went. "Giovanna?" I called quietly.

"Giovanna?" I said, a little louder.

"I am here." I heard a shuffling and Giovanna appeared around the doorframe of Anna's office. She was wearing an elegant purple dress and a string of black pearls. She looked like Sophia Loren's kid sister.

"You have a question?"

"No. I was just making sure you were here."

"Good, then," said Giovanna. "We are quite busy today." She swept back into Anna's office and I slouched into my office across the hall, thumping down into my chair. The counter had a scattering of pens and paper clips and, unaccountably, a pink box of Japanese Pocky sticks. The box of English letters was just where I'd left it yesterday. I plucked out a few letters, reading two or three to get my head into it. I stopped when I came to this one:

Dear Juliet,

There's a boy back home who I think is really special. He's kind and he values his words. He knows what's going on in my mind, and he is genuinely interested about me. He knows I love to cook. And he looks directly in my eyes, even when he's talking in a group. He loves me with his gaze. I've never felt so vulnerable and comfortable at the same time as when he's looking at me.

In all my little-girl daydreams about my wedding day, I could never picture the groom's face—even when I dated other guys. I never saw the face. But now, I see this boy's face at the end of the aisle. He smiles, drawing me closer and closer to my future. And I want that.

I leaned back in my chair and sighed. Yes, I thought. That's what I wanted too. That's what the letters were all about. My own letter was burning in my backpack, begging to be mailed, begging to be answered.

Giovanna called down the hall to say she was going out for a while. I heard the front door open and close and then all was quiet. When I got up a few minutes later to stretch, the man with the canary-yellow tie had also disappeared. I poked my head into Anna's office. The blue of her laptop screen was reflected in her glasses. "Who was that?" I asked.

"Who was who?" She was still looking at the screen.

"The older man."

"You don't know?"

"Wait a minute," I said, "was that Giulio Tamassia?"

"Who else?"

"Wow. So that was—"

"Giovanna's father. Yes." Anna looked like a teacher waiting for her slowest student to catch up. "Giulio started the Club di Giulietta. You should know this. He *is* the Club di Giulietta. He is a very important man."

I knew the facts, just not the face. In 1972, Giulio Tamassia began hosting dinners for his friends, a group of intellectuals—all men—who ate and drank and talked about love and women and politics. They named themselves the Club di Giulietta. In 1989, a city commissioner approached them with the problem of the letters—now hundreds every year—and Giulio offered their services. They would write back to the senders. That's how it all began.

Giulio had done well for himself. He'd started off as a baker. He'd worked his way up to running a large confectionery business, and when he retired, he'd bought an apartment building that had an empty space on the main floor. He decided to set it up as an office, this office, dedicated entirely to the answering of letters to Juliet.

"Maybe I should have introduced myself," I said.

"Probably he is a very busy man," Anna said, giving a last glance at her laptop before closing it down.

"He didn't seem to want to talk," I said meekly.

Anna put two fingers on either side of the rims of her glasses and pushed them up the bridge of her nose. "I told you. He is a very important man. He is good friends with the *sindaco* of Verona, the mayor. Many politicians still call on him for advice. And he was friends with Zeffirelli."

"The movie director? No way."

"Yes, and with Pavarotti."

"Wow."

"Probably he is very important."

———

All through that first winter after Claire returned, I helped her out by picking her up in the mornings and dropping her off at her new job. It was on my way to work, anyway.

Every morning, I ground fresh coffee and brought along a cup for her—black, how she liked it—and she'd take it in her hands to warm them. Morning after morning, I'd drive through the sunrise with her, the frosted windshield sparkling, her hands wrapped around the coffee. "Thank you," she'd say. "I really don't know what I'd do without you."

And then, in the spring, came a surprise. "I've bought a house," she told me. We were driving home. I'd swung by to get her and we were going to go for a walk along the river.

"That's fantastic," I said. "Where's your new place?"

"There," she said, pointing to a house as we drove by it.

I was surprised. It wasn't that far from mine. Now we'd be near enough to walk over to each other's place. Close enough to guarantee we would be spending a whole lot of time together.

It's funny. Research shows that the best predictor for whom you might fall in love with is not physical attraction. It's not height or weight or hormones. It's nothing like that. It's much more simple. The number one predictor of love is proximity. This has been tested over and over. In one study, university researchers mapped out the relationships that developed in a student residence over a semester and there was nearly a one-to-one correlation with how far apart the lovers' rooms were. A massive follow-up study was done for the entire island of Manhattan, geo-teching a thousand relationships. Again, the proximity theory proved true: If you live close to another person, your chances of falling in love with them will skyrocket.

So Claire was moving into my neighborhood. My fate was sealed. There was no sign of a boyfriend—for the first time since I'd known her—and I began to think it could all work out. Maybe, just maybe, she really was the person I would grow old with. And there was nothing more that I wanted.

———

Anna sauntered into my little office later in the morning carrying a Tupperware container of cookies. Soňa had come into the office too, and she edged in behind Anna. Anna plunked the cookies down on my desk.

"Time for a break," Soňa said. "It's an Italian thing."

Anna stifled a smile. "Are we working you too hard, Soňa?"

Soňa pulled the lid off the container and sniffed at the contents.

"What are these?" I asked, examining the cookies.

"Chocolate mint," Anna said. "I baked them last night."

I crunched down on one of them and a flood of pleasure danced across my tongue. "Delicious," I said.

Anna laughed, making a sound like somebody shaking a tambourine.

"Anna," I said, "what's with these Pocky sticks?" I pointed to the little pink box of Japanese treats.

"Those must be Manuela's," she said.

"Have I met her?"

"We are many secretaries," Anna said. "Manuela, she has worked here for many years. Elena, Barbara, there are many."

"But where is everybody?"

"It is August. Everyone in Italy is on holiday, but the letters must still be answered. So Soňa here, she must come every day. Is that not correct, Soňa?"

Soňa performed a mock salute. "Yes, sir."

"Manuela," Anna continued, "says it's good to have young people. They will understand better the hearts of the young people who write to us."

Soňa remained poker-faced.

"Soňa," began Anna again, "is an exchange student—from where? Somewhere near Russia?" I could see Anna was egging her on.

"The Czech Republic," said Soňa. They held their sour faces for a moment, then both broke into wide grins.

"Exchange student?" I asked.

"I am with Erasmus. You know it?"

I did. Erasmus was an exchange program for university students in the EU. "So what are you studying?"

"Languages."

"Ah," I said. "That figures. How many?"

"Italian is my fourth, no, my fifth language."

I studied the girl with her blond ponytail. At least a dozen colorful bracelets dangled from each of her wrists.

"Manuela," continued Anna, "she answers the Japanese letters."

"Is she Japanese?"

"No. But she studied Japanese for some years. This is usually her room."

"Oh," I said.

"Probably you should not eat her Pocky sticks."

"I won't. I haven't touched them."

"Manuela will lead our tours. She is an official guide for the city. It will be good if you can talk to her about your Shakespeare play."

"I'm actually leaving in a few days."

Soňa looked surprised. "But you have only just arrived."

"I know. I have to go back, to teach."

"And for another reason?" Anna prodded.

I looked from one to the other. They had me cornered.

"Did you write your letter yet?" Anna asked.

"What letter?" Soňa asked. "You are writing a letter?"

———

Okay, so I know what you're thinking. The letter. What did I write in my letter to Juliet?

Well, here it is, word for word:

Dear Juliet,

It's been a long journey. I have had my share of broken hearts and I have had romance too. I have traveled the world, but in the end I am still alone.

There is one, Claire, whom I have known for many years. I fell in love with her in the beginning, but it was unrequited. Over the years,

94

we became the closest of friends. I have seen her through long-term boyfriends but now she too is alone.

How shall I tell her a spark is still there? I am too afraid to endanger a long friendship. In this I feel like a foolish schoolboy. Perhaps you have some words of wisdom for me?

It's a bit pretentious, I can see that now. I guess I thought I had to adopt a certain tone with Juliet. *Perhaps you have some words of wisdom for me?* I mean really.

That's what I stuffed into the red letter box in the courtyard across from the statue of Juliet. Juliet of the golden right breast. I imagined Soňa would be by within a day or two to collect the letters, and mine would be among them. I certainly hadn't put my last name on it, so I hoped that no one would recognize it.

There was nothing to do now, except go back to Canada and wait for my answer.

————

Sadia peered up at me. "Do you believe in fate, Mr. Dixon?" I could see that she wasn't intending to challenge me. She was being earnest. "I mean, that Juliet and Romeo are meant for each other. Like, what did you say . . . star-crossed?"

"Sounds kind of dubious," Devin said.

"But look." Sadia turned around in her seat to face Devin. "He met her right when he needed to meet someone. It was like it was meant to be."

Devin harrumphed, but Sadia ignored him. "So what do you believe, Mr. Dixon?" she repeated.

"Well," I said, "I can't say I believe in fate. I think we are the architects of our own misfortune." I don't know where that came from. "As far as love goes," I fumbled on, "I don't think there's only one person for you in the whole wide world and that you have to go and find them. I don't think it's like that. Sometimes love is something you have to work at. Sometimes it takes a long time."

I could see from the expressions on the faces of my students that most of them didn't agree with me. Young people are hopeless romantics.

"Okay," I said, trying a different tack. "Why don't we see what Shakespeare has to say? Right after the balcony scene, Romeo declares his love for Juliet to Friar Lawrence. He's quite suddenly forgotten all about Rosaline and now, he's madly in love with Juliet."

"Okay." Sadia eyed me warily.

"*Wisely and slow*, says Friar Lawrence, *they stumble that run fast*."

"Meaning?"

"That young people like you shouldn't go all crazy over love. You shouldn't rush into it."

"So, don't fall in love at first sight?" Sadia said.

"Well, maybe, but the point is—"

"But Romeo and Juliet *did* fall in love," she insisted. "They *are* crazy about each other."

"Yes, but . . ." I stopped and rallied. "Listen," I said, "Romeo and Juliet are playing with fire here. They're going to die for this love. The friar can almost see it coming, so he's asking: Is it worth it?"

I'd meant these to be rhetorical questions, but Sadia nodded savagely. "Yes," she insisted. "Yes."

"Maybe they can make it work," I said. "That's exactly what Friar Lawrence is starting to think—that maybe their love can end the fighting between the families. Look here, he talks to them both in scene 6. *Love moderately*, he says. *Long love doth so*."

A few of the students shook their heads, not understanding.

"It means you have to be careful about love. It means you should take it slowly. The kind of love that lasts a lifetime isn't about good looks. It's about more than hormones, more than, I don't know, pheromones."

"Mr. Dixon," Devin said, "can I ask you a serious question?"

Devin, being serious. That surprised me.

"Why do we have to study all this stuff. It's so old I mean, if this book is four hundred years old, then what's in it for us?"

"Ah," I said. "Good question."

"Well?"

"I think, Devin, we study Shakespeare because what he says is universally, perennially true even after all this time."

Devin leaned back in his desk again, but he nodded to show that he thought that was a pretty good answer. "Okay," he said, "so what happens next?"

———

I'd be flying home the following day. I'd thought a lot about love on this trip and I was happy to at least have written a letter, even if it was mostly symbolic. Maybe I wouldn't even receive an answer. Maybe the writing of it was enough—just to fling it out into the universe like a wish. Maybe that was enough.

I walked through the streets with Soña, up to the new office on Vicola Santa Cecilia. Anna wasn't coming this afternoon. It was just the two of us going to meet Veronica. I couldn't help but ask Soña how she'd gotten into all this.

"Do you have some kind of special interest in love?"

Soña pulled to a stop. "Doesn't everyone have an interest in love?"

We were passing by the street where Juliet's house was—you could tell by the crowds we had to push through.

"I suppose so," I said. "But don't you worry about giving advice to all these people?"

"Sometimes I answer these letters by saying love cannot be defined. It can only be felt," Soña said. "In this way, I don't give a direct answer."

"It's like a loophole," I said.

"Loophole?"

"Never mind. That's good. Is it okay if I use that?"

Soňa tipped her head. "As you like."

The lane past Juliet's house opened onto the Piazza delle Erbe, the old vegetable market. Between the fountains and statues, there are still stalls, but now they're mostly filled with tourist souvenirs. Only a couple of the stalls carry golden jars of honey or sheaves of fennel. In the middle of the square is a fountain whose pedestal looks like a giant wheel of cheese. Mounted on top of it is the statue of a woman. The torso is actually from the Roman era, with long, draping folds carved into the marble; the head is medieval; and the arms hold a scroll upon which is written the motto of the city—THE DEFENDER OF JUSTICE AND THE LOVER OF HONOR.

Across the square, Veronica skipped toward us, a broad and toothy grin on her face. Veronica was the youngest of Juliet's secretaries—by far. She was still a teenager—still in school, in fact—and she lived on the very outskirts of Verona in one of the far-off suburbs. She'd caught the bus to meet us.

"*Ciao,*" she said, bouncing into step with us.

Across from where we were walking, midway up on the opposite side of the square, a narrow lane jutted north between two buildings, and an archway, like the Bridge of Sighs in Venice, ran between the two, a couple of stories off the ground. Inexplicably, a massive curved shape hung beneath the archway from a chain. "Veronica," I said, "what is that thing?"

"A dinosaur bone," she said. "That's what we tell the tourists."

Soňa flashed her a warning look.

"Okay, but what is it really?"

"The rib bone of a whale. They found it when they built this square, maybe five hundred years ago, maybe longer."

"But why is it hanging there?"

"Because we are all mad."

"Excuse me?"

"We have a saying here: '*Venesiani gran sion, Padoani tuti doton, Vicentini maia gati, Veronesi tuti mati.*' It's in dialect," said Veronica. "It means Venetians are grand sirs, high class," she said, performing a little flourish with her hand, "and people from Padua are all doctors. People from Vicenza eat cats," continued Veronica.

"Eat cats?" I said.

"And people from Verona are all mad." Veronica laughed.

"That explains a few things," said Soňa.

"It's funny," I said, "in English, we often talk about love being madness."

Soňa studied me.

"We're always saying things like, 'I'm crazy about her,' or, 'She drives me out of my mind.' Even Shakespeare, in *Romeo and Juliet*, calls love '*a madness most discreet.*'"

"It is kind of crazy," Soňa said.

"It is the same in Italian," said Veronica. "*Sono pazza di te.*"

Soňa pursed her lips together and nodded sagely. They both turned to me.

"Why are you not learning Italian?" Veronica asked. "You are here."

"I don't know." I was too embarrassed to say that I'd opened my grammar book exactly once since I'd arrived. It intimidated me. *Prego!* the cover announced, *An Invitation to Italian.* Inside the book, my friend's name, Desiree, had been written in looping blue letters on the flyleaf. Desiree had gone on to do her master's degree in interpreting and translation, and I knew she was hoping I'd pick up some of the language while I was here. Boy, was she going to be disappointed.

I had flipped through the first few pages and learned bits of the opening chapter on introducing yourself—but beyond that, it seemed impossible for me to learn this most mellifluous of languages from the pages of a book.

"I guess," I said, "understanding has always come slowly for me."

———

I walked with Soña and Veronica up the Corso Porta Borsari, the wide cobblestone street that runs perpendicularly off from the square. A few blocks up, Soña ducked around a corner into the lane called Vicolo Santa Cecilia.

Soña sprang ahead of us and rattled at the front door with her key. She stepped through and held the front door for us. Inside, we tramped up the marble stairs and crossed over to the glassed-in entrance of the new office. Soña had that key too.

We'd left a pile of letters in the middle of the table the last time we were here, and we each took our seats as if we were sitting down to a card game. Papers rustled as we opened envelopes. Soña drew out a large sheet of paper and her face twisted into disgust. The paper had an imprint of lipstick on it where someone had kissed it. Soña held it up between her forefinger and thumb like something rank. "Listen to this one," she said. "'When the stars cross the moon, I will see you soon.'"

"That's terrible," I said.

"Terrible," she agreed. "Stars don't cross in front of the moon. Who writes these things?" She bent to pen her response and shook her head. "Sometimes, I just want to slap these people."

"And," Veronica said, "how about this one? 'Dear Juliet,'" she read. "'I'm Ellie from Kentucky. I have a lover. I really love him. I know he is not perfect. But his imperfections are just perfect for me.'"

"That's nice," I said.

"No, no . . . listen," said Veronica. "'The problem is I am not a good girlfriend. I like drinking and I have lots of problems. I drink without control. I mess up with other boys. I want to fix it and be a good girl. But it's not that easy. I have already broken his heart many times. I'm on vacation, traveling in Europe for twenty-six days. After I come back home, I wish I could be a nice, good person. Thanks for reading.'" Veronica looked up. "What do you think?"

"Get off the sauce, Ellie," I said.

"Sauce?" asked Veronica.

"The booze, the alcohol."

Veronica looked pensive.

"What amazes me," I pushed on, "is that none of these people seem to see the obvious in their predicaments."

"I think," said Veronica, "that is why they write. They write not just to Juliet . . ."

"They write to themselves," finished Soňa. "They write to make it clear to themselves."

I tapped the pen to my lips. "Maybe," I said. "Maybe."

———

I had a key to Claire's place and she had a key to mine. We'd water the plants and pick up the mail if the other was away. One day I popped over and she didn't answer the door when I knocked. There was a pause and then, "C'mon in," she called. Her voice sounded distant, coming from upstairs somewhere. I squeaked open the front door.

"Where are you?"

"Up here."

I clumped up the stairs.

She was in the kitchen, crouched on top of the stove in an odd position. I rushed forward. "What the hell . . . what are you doing?"

She grunted. "I'm trying to put in this new stove cover." Above the stove, she held up a stove hood with one hand and one knee. In her other hand was a screwdriver.

"Here," I said, "let me get this. Why didn't you call me?"

"Because I was holding up this."

"Okay, look, here . . ." I held the stove hood in place and she turned the first screw into place and tightened it. Gradually, screw by screw, we secured it into place.

"Can you help me off here?" she asked. She reached out a hand.

She was folded up quite extraordinarily. "I've been here a while," she said.

I helped her down and she stretched her neck once, stood back to survey her work. "It looks good though, don't you think?"

"Sure."

"You wouldn't believe how much that thing costs."

"Don't even tell me."

Claire had been in her place for a while now, gradually making it her own. She had expensive taste, that's for sure. She carried a red designer purse around, a Louis Vuitton, I think. She wore smart little black dresses and had her blond hair trimmed in a swank salon. One day, she showed me a door handle she wanted to install at her place. It cost over three hundred dollars. But it's a door handle, I thought, and not even for the front door. "Won't you need a whole bunch of them?" I said, "One for each room in your—"

"But feel it," she said, placing the cold brass into my hand. I held it in my palm. "Impeccable," I said. I knew she liked the word, but she yanked the door handle away from me, thinking I was making fun of her.

"I might have to hire someone to do the renovations," she said. "This is getting to be too much."

"Yeah," I said, "that might be the way to go. But it'll cost you. It will cost a lot."

———

"Ecco!" *Veronica said. "Here is a* letter about Shakespeare."

"What does it say?"

"It's in Italian." She translated it for me. "'*Cara Juliet,*'" she began. "'Why do you wish to kill yourself? Why do you and Romeo stay in Verona? Why do you not run away from there?'"

That exact question had in fact come up in class, and I didn't really have a good answer for it.

102

"In my opinion," said Veronica, "you cannot know what it is like for another person. Maybe it is a good option for us—to run away—but maybe it is not possible for her."

"For a young woman in that time," I said.

"Maybe for a young woman in any time," said Soňa.

We were quiet again after that. In my peripheral vision, I saw Soňa stop at one letter. She stared at it, then reached back for the last one she had answered. She placed them side by side.

"Look at this," said Soňa. "This one is from a father and this one"—Soňa held up the one beside it—"is from his daughter. Both from the same address." Soňa pushed them across the table toward me. "You can answer these."

"Why me?"

"Because you're older. Because you're a man."

"Yes, but . . .why—"

"Take them," insisted Soňa.

I sighed and reached for the letters.

The father wrote that his wife of twenty-three years had left him. "There was a lot of change," he wrote. "We had good years, but we became different in character. Then she lied to the children, our daughters." He went on, "I said to my wife, 'If you no longer love me then by all means leave, but beware the impact on the children.' And now she has had three relationships in two years. I don't know what to say to my daughters. I worry so much that they will become cynical, that they will never be able to love."

The daughter's letter was even more difficult. Her name was Rebecca and she was the eldest at sixteen. "They say time is a good healer," she began. "My parents got divorced two years ago, but my heart is still broken. Is it possible to have a broken heart when the breakup wasn't mine? Mother has a new partner and seems happy, but my father is so very lonely."

I wondered if they'd sat down together to write these letters as a way to try to heal. But I don't think they'd read each other's letters. So much sorrow. So many secrets.

Soňa was watching me.

"What am I supposed to say?" I asked.

"Maybe," Veronica started, "you can say that they both have someone who loves them very much. You can tell the father how much his daughter cares about him and you can tell the daughter how much she is loved by her father."

"Yes," I said. "I suppose that's a start."

At the end of the day, Soňa walked back to the university, where she shared a flat with another exchange student. Veronica had to catch her bus home, so I walked with her down to her stop. It was on my way anyway.

"You are leaving soon?" she asked with a sideways glance.

"Yes, tomorrow."

"You have not been here long."

"No." I didn't know what else to say. We turned left onto the busy Corso Cavour. "Veronica," I said, as we walked, "I can't help but ask. How old are you exactly?"

"Almost seventeen." She jutted out her dimpled chin.

"And you're answering letters?"

"Why not? I like it."

"Fair enough. But how did you become a Secretary di Giulietta?"

We came to her stop at the Piazzetta Santi Apostoli and stood in the shade of a towering marble statue, of a politician maybe, who stared impassively out over the square with a pigeon fluttering on his head. "One time, I went with a school group and they showed us what they do at the Club di Giulietta. They told us that they always need help, so then I returned later, by myself, to answer the letters. I am helping since then."

"Well, good for you. They need help."

"And you? You will come back?" she asked.

"I don't know. I'd like to."

"Anna said you wrote a letter."

"Word travels fast."

Veronica waited for me to say more.

"It's complicated," I said. "It's kind of complicated."

———

The next morning, Saturday, I went into the club, and the only person there was Giovanna. She was sitting behind the reception desk. She looked harried.

"Ah," she said, when I came in through the door. "You are leaving today, are you not?"

"Yes, I have a train this afternoon, to Milano." I stopped just behind the circular table at the front. Someone had painted the top with a mural of a big red heart. I hadn't noticed before, probably because it was usually covered in letters.

Giovanna rose, patting down her dress. "I want to thank you for answering the letters here."

"I didn't really do that much."

She held up a hand like a stop sign. "Every letter helps," she said. "It is too much for us alone."

"I just wanted to say goodbye before I left."

Giovanna smiled. "Would you like a ride to the train station?"

"I've left my bags at the hotel. I have to go get them first."

"That is not a problem. We can stop there."

Giovanna swept around the desk. She already had keys in her hand. I stood still.

"Are you coming?" she said.

"Yes, yes . . . of course."

We headed to her car. I tucked myself into the front seat and we puttered off down the road to my hotel.

"You are staying where?"

"Still at the same hotel, not far from the train station."

105

"Yes, yes, I remember." She eyed the rearview mirror again. "It would have been good for you to stay in a flat. Many people here have started these B and Bs. The economy now is not so good. People are trying to make extra money."

"That's doesn't sound mad to me," I said.

She turned to me. "Mad?"

"Oh, you know, the saying that the Veronese are all mad."

"Who told you that?"

"I . . . ah . . . it was because of the whale bone hanging in the Piazza delle Erbe."

"There is another story about the whale bone," she said.

"That it's a dinosaur bone?"

"No. The story tells that the bone will finally fall when an honest person walks underneath it. It must be a person who has never told a lie."

I'd walked under that archway a dozen times.

"And it's been up there for, what, five hundred years?"

"Sì."

We drove over the bridge. The Roman arena came into view. Giovanna tipped her head forward, eyes glancing up at the sky. Over the arena, a line of black clouds was unfurling in the distance.

"The sky," she said, "is preparing something for tomorrow."

"I'll be gone," I said, but she didn't seem to be listening. She turned left, and we passed through one of the old medieval gates, the one with the placard bolted up onto the stones THERE IS NO WORLD WITHOUT VERONA'S WALLS.

"It was nice to see your father the other day," I blurted.

"Yes, he asked who you were."

"What did you tell him?"

"That you were Canadian. That you were trying to help."

Trying.

She waited outside the hotel while I grabbed my bags; then she took me to the train station. She pulled up in front of the doors there.

"Well," I said, "it was nice to meet you. Thanks for letting me answer the letters."

She nodded once, then pierced me with a hard look. "I hope," she said, "you have found what you were looking for."

"I . . . um . . . yes, thanks."

"Then," she said, "I will say goodbye."

I hopped out of the car and yanked my bags from the backseat. Giovanna was already staring ahead. "Goodbye, then," I said. *"Ciao."*

She pulled away and I heaved my bag into the dark of the train station. I still had an hour to kill, so I sat on a wooden bench, watching a screen that showed the trains arriving and departing, the plastic letters and times cascading over and gradually shuffling up to the top of the list; Firenze, Venezia, Genova, and finally Milano.

From Milano, hours later, my plane lifted up over the Alps, snow still lacing the highest peaks, dark valleys and shimmering lakes appearing between the mountaintops. Far below us a river wound like a ribbon of silver and on one green slope, a tiny perfect village sat like a toy model.

And then we were in the clouds. The pilot said we would be flying over Paris and then out over the English Channel, but I couldn't see a thing. Eventually, the sky purpled and darkened. A single star winked on above the banks of clouds, and I settled back in my seat for the long journey home.

Act Two

5

I am fortune's fool

I have a black metal mailbox outside my front door. I usually open it to bank statements and flyers from questionable pizza establishments, but I came home one evening with a satchel full of papers to be graded and saw that there was a letter waiting for me. I knew what it was immediately, having stuffed several hundred letters myself into exactly the same kind of envelope. In the bottom corner was the familiar graphic of Juliet, hair tossed in the wind, hand outstretched imploringly, a look of utter desolation on her face.

I took the envelope inside, impressed that it had traveled six thousand miles to find me. For some time, I held it in my hand like an emcee about to announce the winner at an awards show. I'd been waiting for this for months and now it was here, the answer to my question.

The answer was short, but it was thoughtful and practical, not unlike something I might have written myself.

"Dear Glenn," it read.

Love coming out of long friendship is the most genuine kind of love. If you have known this woman for a long time, you also know what she likes. Take her out to her favorite place and confess her your feelings. Maybe she is just waiting for you. Wishing you the best luck.

Juliet

I was thrilled. I couldn't tell who had written the letter—maybe someone I knew—but it didn't matter.

It meant something to get a letter. It meant hope.

Certainly there wasn't any earth-shattering advice there—nothing I hadn't thought of before—it was more that I hoped the letter itself could be a catalyst. In the months since I'd left Verona, I'd thought a lot about this, and I'd come up with a plan. I would show the letter to Claire.

She knew about my trip to Verona, of course, but I'd tell her the whole story. I'd tell her about the boxes of letters. I'd tell her about all the broken hearts. Then I'd confess to her that I'd written my own letter. I would tell her that I'd posted it in the red letter box in the courtyard at Juliet's house; then I'd pull out Juliet's answer and it would astonish her. Suddenly, she'd realize how much I loved her. And then, of course, she'd tell me how much she loved me back. And not just as a friend. Then I'd take Claire back to Italy, to revisit the Gates of Paradise, properly this time. Maybe I'd have the plane tickets all ready. It would bowl her over. I would actually learn to speak some Italian and maybe we would go to Verona, where we would stand on the balcony and blow kisses to the adoring crowds.

That was the plan. That's what I imagined would happen.

_____

The school furnace kicked in with a dusty thump and my students, their arms full of books, slouched into the classroom. There is always a point in the school year when things have become so mundane and so routine that everyone, teachers included, are going only through the motions, effectively numb.

Outside, the athletic fields were covered in snow. A gray sky hung over the city. Andy walked in with Allison. I'd seen them at her locker, chatting and leaning in to each other. They'd been walking between classes together for a few weeks now, and Andy grinned at me when he came in. I nodded back, then signaled for him to take his seat.

"All right," I began. "Today is the wedding scene, one of the shortest scenes in the whole play." I paused for effect. "You'd think Shakespeare would have spent a little more time on it."

Devin mumbled something and kicked errantly at the metal leg of his chair.

"Why do you think it's so short?" I asked. "Could it be a lie?"

Sadia's eyes narrowed. "What's that supposed to mean?"

"That maybe the wedding was a sham. Act 2, scene 5. It's only two pages long."

A rustle of pages swept down the rows. Sadia stared at me. She was trying to puzzle out where I was going with this.

"Certain scholars have suggested that Friar Lawrence botched the wedding on purpose, that he left some part of it out, you know, that it wasn't legal."

"Why?"

"The two families are at war. It's been going on for so long that I don't think anyone even remembers how it started. Maybe Friar Lawrence is starting to realize how hard it will be to break that cycle. And things have heated up again. Tybalt is on the warpath. Tybalt has sent a letter to Romeo asking for a duel."

Devin was still kicking at the metal leg of his chair—*clack, clack, clack*. I wasn't sure how long I could keep their interest today.

"*Senza indirizzo*," I said.

"What?" said Sadia.

"It literally means 'without an address,' and all through the play, there are letters that don't get to where they're supposed to be. They mess everything up. But let's go back a bit," I said. "Who actually proposed here?"

Sadia tilted her head to one side. "The balcony scene," she said. "Juliet asks Romeo to marry her."

Devin stopped his tapping.

"But don't you think that's weird?" I asked. "The girl asking the boy?"

"You already said Romeo is a bit of a wimp," Devin said.

"I didn't say he was a wimp. I said he was naïve. But think, why would Juliet ask Romeo, rather than the other way around?"

At least everyone was looking at me, trying to puzzle it out. "It's because," I said, "she's already in an arranged marriage and she needs to get out of it. This is her ticket out."

Sadia went instantly pale. Her hand was trembling. She reached up and pulled her hijab lower over her forehead. She didn't say anything for the rest of the class.

Something was wrong. Something was dreadfully wrong.

The next day, Sadia was even more distant. She opened her textbook but would not raise her eyes from the book.

"Today," I said, "let's begin with Mercutio. He's Romeo's friend. He's a hothead and a loudmouth."

"Sounds familiar," said Allison under her breath. A few of the kids tittered and glanced over at Devin.

"Mercutio," I pushed on, "is spoiling for a fight. He's just come into the square and he has a few other guys with him."

"Like a gang?" Andy asked. Andy still wore his rugby jacket, though the season was long over.

"Yes," I said, "like a gang. *For now, these hot days, is the mad blood stirring.*"

Andy's neck muscles tightened and he edged forward, eager for the action to begin.

"And then the Capulet boys enter from the other end of the square. Tybalt is strutting like a rooster."

"They're going to fight," said Devin. He balled his hands into fists on his desk.

"But Romeo is nowhere to be seen. He's still at the church, getting married."

"Oh man," said Andy.

"So Mercutio steps up but Tybalt's still asking for Romeo. He'd sent a letter asking for a duel, remember? But Mercutio taunts him and says, '*Any man that can write may answer a letter.*'"

Andy looked confused. "Mercutio's going to answer the letter?"

"It means he's going to fight him," said Devin. "That's his answer."

"Exactly," I said. "So, let's do this. Devin," I said, "how's about you come up here?"

Devin hoisted himself up gamely.

"And Andy." Andy startled and then shuffled up beside me, and I handed him the yardstick. Devin stood on my other side and I handed him an old black umbrella I'd found in the staff room.

"Are you serious?" Devin asked, giving the umbrella a twirl.

"Now," I said, gazing across the sea of faces. "I need a third. I need a Romeo. Sadia?"

Her eyes were lowered and her mouth was taut. "Um, Mr. Dixon," she said, "maybe can I not do this today?"

"Okay," I said. I searched the classroom again. Most of the students tucked their heads down to avoid eye contact with me. "Minh," I said. "How about you?"

Minh was an English as a Second Language student from Vietnam. The counselors had put him in my class because they couldn't fill his time block with anything else. The principal knew Minh wasn't ready for my English class, but there weren't many other options. Poor Minh. He was a good kid—unassuming—and when I addressed him in class he usually had a goofy grin on his face that meant he didn't understand a damn thing I was saying. He understood his name, though, and he gaped at me, terrified. "C'mon up," I said. "I'll show you what to do."

His slow march to the front of class was excruciating. Some of the other kids were snickering, but I shot them a don't-you-dare look and they quickly shut up. Minh hunched between the other two boys, and I handed him a wooden ruler.

"Okay. Devin, you're Tybalt, and Andy, you're going to be Mercutio. You guys are fighting but not that seriously. More like sparring, you understand?"

Devin raised his umbrella and gave it a swoosh through the air.

"Good," I said. "Now Andy—I mean Mercutio—have a go at him."

I let them parry through a few thrusts and deflections. Both had seen enough movies to perform a pretty decent mock sword fight.

"Okay, Minh. Now, it's your turn."

Minh looked at me helplessly, gripping the ruler in both hands like a bouquet of flowers.

Devin glared at Minh. "Doesn't he want to fight?"

"No, Romeo doesn't. In fact, he tries to talk Tybalt down."

"Okay," I said. "Let's slow this way down." I turned to the class. "Watch closely. This part is important."

Devin swung his umbrella in a slow motion through the air. Andy, at a quarter speed, raised the yardstick to deflect it.

"Great," I said. "Now Romeo steps forward," I gave Minh a little push. "Romeo tries to stop the fight," I said, steering Minh around so that he was facing Mercutio. "He says, *Gentlemen, for shame . . .*"

"*Shame*," Minh tried.

"Right, and then he raises his sword to stop them, but he only blocks Mercutio's sword." I worked all three of them like puppets. "Tybalt is expecting Mercutio to block his next thrust, you see, but Romeo gets in the way."

"And Tybalt skewers Mercutio," Devin said, pushing his sword forward between Andy's arm and torso—sideways to the class—so that it appeared as if he really were stabbing Andy.

"Do you see?" I said. "Romeo blocked Mercutio, and Tybalt's sword kept going, right through Mercutio."

Andy fell to the ground, flailing. Minh stared at him, then back at me. I gave him a wink.

"And now Tybalt runs off." I gestured to Devin, who looked a bit disappointed that his part was over. "And Mercutio dies uttering the famous curse."

"*A plague on both your houses,*" said Andy from the floor.

"Excellent."

"Houses?" said Minh.

"It means a curse on both the families."

Minh nodded and for once, I think he actually understood.

I turned to Sadia. This was the most important scene in the book, a real turning point, but I seemed to have lost her. There was a distance in her eyes and her lower lip was on the verge of trembling.

"You guys can sit down now," I said. "And Minh?"

Minh turned.

"You did great," I said. "Good job."

The bell went just then, jangling through the silence. I wanted to speak to Sadia, to ask her what was wrong, but she scooped up her books, tucked her head down, and barged out the door at almost a run.

———

Sadia wasn't in class the following day. It was a Wednesday, a Wednesday morning, and they were the worst. No one was really awake. I had a big mug of coffee sitting near me on the table at the front of class. On days like these, I sat on the table, not even bothering to stand.

The students were quiet. The light slanting through the windows was tender, almost fragile. At the back of the class, some teacher had put up posters. They'd been there for a long time. One of them was that one with Garfield the cat, where he's clinging with two paws to a tree branch. HANG IN THERE, it read.

Devin sat slumped, his eyes heavy with sleep. I don't think he'd quite clued in to the fact that the day had started.

"This is the part," I began, "where everything changes. This is where everything goes off the rails."

Devin propped himself up. "What goes off the rails?"

"Absolutely everything. Mercutio is dead and Romeo goes berserk."

"Berserk?" Devin perked up even more.

"Romeo," I went on, "chases down Tybalt. He's almost insane with rage and he stabs Tybalt through the heart. He kills him."

Devin nodded, impressed.

"And then," I said, "Romeo looks down at Tybalt's dead body and suddenly realizes what he's done. He realizes he's just lost everything—Juliet, Verona, everything. But it's too late. It's done. It's happened, and he says one of the greatest lines in the whole play."

I waited a beat, then boomed out the line in my best theatrical voice. "*O, I am fortune's fool.*"

"Jeez," said Devin. "That's pretty good."

"Romeo flees." I shook my head. "It's a mess. The cobblestones are spattered with blood. And Prince Escalus emerges from his palace to—"

Andy put up his hand.

"Yes, Andy?"

"Where's Sadia?" he asked.

A few heads swiveled, looking for her.

"Sadia's not here today."

"But Sadia is always the Prince," Andy said. "Is she sick?"

"I don't know where she—" I saw the eyes questioning me. "I'm sure she'll be back soon."

"So," I started again, "who wants to play the Prince?"

"We should wait for Sadia," Andy insisted.

"Look," I said, "I'll be the Prince until she gets back." I stared them down and continued. "Prince Escalus rushes out into the square. People are bustling in from all sides. In the movie version, they carry in the bodies of Mercutio and Tybalt and lay them out, right there on the bloody cobblestones."

I could feel their attention turn toward the story again.

"You have to remember," I plowed on, "the Montagues and Capulets have been fighting for so long that no one even remembers how it all started. The hate is ingrained in their thinking; it's not rational, and now . . . and now there's this."

Allison looked up from her text. "Nobody meant for this to happen," she said.

"That's right. But it did happen. Two people are dead and Romeo makes a run for it."

"Oh shit," said Devin.

"Devin!" I cast him a warning look.

"Mr. Dixon. C'mon. This is intense."

"Yes, it is. This is where the disaster begins."

———

I recommended a guy to Claire. Someone who could do some renovations on her house. A teacher friend of mine had a husband who did all sorts of handyman work. Let's call him Rick. He came by with his tape measures and toolboxes, wearing a baseball cap and a hoodie, and in no time at all, he was over at Claire's place daily, tearing out floorboards, replacing the patio doors, painting and sawing and nailing. What started out as a couple of odd jobs turned into a major enterprise and weeks became months.

I went over one evening and the stairs and floors were draped in canvas sheets, duct-taped down, paint-spattered and dusty. I heard the sound of a table saw ripping through wood in the garage. The blade was screaming.

Claire sat alone in her kitchen. She looked pale.

"Are you okay?" I asked.

"Not really. I went in to work this morning and I started feeling horrible. Finally, I just came home."

"You don't look so good."

"I feel a little better now." She held a hand on her stomach. "I haven't done anything all day.

"Twenty-four-hour flu?"

"Yeah, maybe. It came on really quickly."

"Well," I said, taking a mock step backward, "I hope it's not catching."

"No," she said. "I don't think you have to worry about that."

The saw started again in the garage. "How long is he going to be here?" I asked. The clock on her stove said it was already after eight o'clock at night.

"I guess until he's finished," she said. "I don't know."

———

When Sadia didn't turn up to class for the second day in a row, I called the main office. I was transferred through to one of the guidance counselors, Jane. "Can I trust you to be discreet?" she asked me.

"Of course. What's happened?"

"Well," she said, "apparently Sadia went to Mrs. Bell, her biology teacher. I think Sadia was more comfortable talking with a female teacher."

"More comfortable about what? What's going on?"

"Sadia's father has arranged a marriage for her."

I was struck silent for a moment.

"Glenn, I have to ask that you not speak with the other students about this. We are dealing with it."

"But is she okay?"

"Mrs. Bell said she was pretty distraught."

"We've been reading *Romeo and Juliet*," I said.

There was a silence on the other end.

"Juliet is in a forced marriage." I said, explaining. "Sadia freaked out a little when we came to that scene. God, I didn't know."

I heard her exhale, almost a sigh, on the other end of the line. "Oh."

"Have you spoken with Sadia?" I asked. "Is she agreeing to this marriage?"

"Glenn," said Jane, "we're dealing with it. I've put in a call to our cultural liaison worker. He's going over there to see the family."

"Okay," I said. "That's good, isn't it?"

"It's a delicate situation. I hope you can appreciate that."

"Of course."

"We're doing what we can. You just hang tight and I'll let you know what happens."

I hung up and wondered if there was anything else I could do. It wasn't the first time arranged marriages had come up in my teaching career. A few years before, I'd dealt with the same thing, only in that case, the student was quite happy about the arrangement. That particular student had told me that no one on earth loved her more than her father and that she trusted him to make a good match for her. Maybe you've heard the statistics. Often arranged marriages are more successful—or more long-lasting at least—than those in the West. Often, they last longer than marriages predicated on what we think is love.

I tried to be a good teacher. I followed the latest trends in educational research and I tried to make my classes engaging. I wanted the students to think for themselves, and I was beginning to think we'd buried ourselves in this reading of the play for too long. I needed to shake things up.

"So . . ." I began, the next day, a Friday, when the students had shuffled in and taken their seats. Sadia wasn't back yet and her empty desk was distressing. I tried to ignore it.

"I've had an idea," I said. "It's going to be fun."

Devin squinted up at me suspiciously.

"We're going to put Romeo on trial for the murder of Tybalt. Close up your books."

The students looked from one to another, shuffling in their desks. A few closed their books, wondering what was going on.

"I'm going to need four volunteers," I said

Predictable groans sounded around the classroom.

"Okay, okay," I said, holding up my hands. "I'll sweeten the deal. If you volunteer, I will erase your worst mark from my mark book—you choose."

Devin's hand shot up like a rocket.

"You don't even know what I'm going to say, Devin."

"Yeah, but I'll do it."

"Okay," I said. "You're on then. We're going to have an actual court case. Devin, you can be the prosecutor—but you're going to need a partner. And I'll need two more volunteers to be the lawyers for the defense team. Allison, how about you?"

Allison pursed her lips in distaste. But she didn't say no. In fact, I'd deliberately asked her because she'd once expressed an interest in going to law school. She thought for a moment then tipped her head in agreement.

"Great. So, Allison, who do you want for your partner?"

Andy straightened a bit in his chair but she looked past him. "Can I have Nancy?" she said. Nancy was a quiet girl who sat nearer to the back. Her marks were high and even Andy knew that Allison had made the right choice.

"Is that okay, Nancy?" I said.

Allison gave her a smile of encouragement, and Nancy nodded her assent.

"Okay, then. You two will be the defense team for Romeo. You're the Montague lawyers."

I gazed around the room. "And who wants to work with Devin?" I said. "Come on. It should be easy. You all saw what happened. We acted it out."

"Jeez, Mr. Dixon," said Devin, "I'm not sure about this."

"You already played Tybalt up here. You want to put his killer on trial?"

"Objection," said Allison, flinging her hand into the air.

"Allison, we haven't even started yet."

"I know," she said, "but you can't call him a killer before we've even started the trial. You're biasing the jury."

Devin glared at Allison. "I have to go against her?"

"That's right."

He sighed. "Fine," he said. "I'll do it."

"And for your partner?"

At the far back of the class sat Marc, the tough kid. Marc usually wore a dirty jean jacket like something from an '80s teen movie. His hair was greasy. And I knew from his file that he'd been in trouble a lot. He was the kind of kid that was barely a step away from jail. He was staring at me with an expression I hadn't seen before.

"Marc," I said, "how about you?"

Devin turned in his desk and his eyes brightened at the choice. "Yeah," he said. "Marc. How about it?"

Devin and Marc, I thought. This was going to be interesting.

The evenings began to warm and lengthen, and Claire and I took long walks along the river pathway, the silver water gurgling down from the mountains with the snowmelt. I hadn't told her about the letter just yet. I was waiting for the right moment. On one walk, almost home, Claire was quiet and pensive. "Do you ever regret not having kids?" she asked.

"It's not that I never wanted kids. It just never happened."

"But do you regret it now?"

"I guess," I said. "I'm a little afraid of growing old alone."

She stopped then. "But you'll have me kicking around," she said.

I remember that clearly. I remember the look on her face—it's just that I didn't know what was behind it. I didn't know what was coming and, really, it didn't matter. That moment hung in the air like a rainbow in a lawn sprinkler. It was a lovely one.

I wish I'd had the letter right then. I wish I could have shaken it out of my back pocket right then and there. But it wouldn't have changed anything.

There'd been some odd things going on. Her renovations were several months along with no end in sight, and Rick, the handyman, was there all the time. Once, and maybe it was nothing, I was driving home and happened to glance down a pathway into a green space between the houses. I could see Claire's back deck through there and I saw, quite clearly, that Rick and Claire were sitting at her patio table. In that instant I remember thinking: Why isn't he working? What is he doing out there with her?

What a fool I am. I didn't clue in at all.

———

I'd given my volunteer students the weekend to examine the evidence and prepare their cases. On Monday morning, I had the two teams stand up at the front of the classroom. I'd pulled my chair away from the teacher's desk and sat in it, as the Prince, presiding over the courtroom.

Allison unloaded a sheaf of papers and books onto the table at the front. Nancy sat beside her. Devin hadn't brought anything up, nor had Marc. They eyed Allison's papers and grimaced at each other.

"Okay," I said, "here's the deal. Each team gets a short opening statement, and then you can call up witnesses."

"Can we call up Mercutio's ghost?" Marc asked.

"Interesting idea," I said. "But no. Let's keep this as real as possible."

Allison began her opening argument. "I submit to the court," she began, "that the Prince had, in fact, decreed that the penalty for fighting in the streets is death." She paused meaningfully. "Tybalt and Mercutio were fighting in the streets, so it follows that Mercutio got the death sentence from Tybalt, and Tybalt then, logically, received the death sentence from Romeo. It was just as the Prince wished."

"That's a load of bull," said Devin. "You can't just take the law into your own hands. Any idiot knows that."

"Devin," I said, "you're making a good point, but you can't speak like that in a court of law."

"But Mr. Dixon—"

"Just make your argument," I sighed.

"Okay. It's crap. Romeo isn't, like, the police or something. He wasn't following the Prince's orders. He just screwed up. He murdered Tybalt and then he ran away."

"Objection," said Allison. She reached down to the table and lifted a small leather-bound book.

"What's that?" I asked.

"This," she began in a solemn tone, "is the Criminal Code of Canada."

"Where did you get that?" Marc asked.

"From Mrs. Ferguson in the library." Allison cleared her throat and continued, "According to part 8, section 232, culpable homicide of the code, first-degree murder has to be planned."

"Okay," Devin blustered, "so second-degree. All right? It's second-degree murder."

"I wasn't finished," Allison said. She opened the book and read, tracing down the paragraphs with her fingertip. "Culpability may be reduced to manslaughter if the person who committed it did so in the heat of passion caused by sudden provocation." She looked up. "It was manslaughter, not even second-degree murder."

Devin whirled on the class. "Wait. You saw Minh kill me. You saw it. How can you say he didn't kill me?" Devin was quite worked up, hopping from foot to foot.

"I'm just saying," Allison said, "that it's not first-degree murder. It's not even second-degree murder." She tapped again on the criminal code. "It's a clear case of manslaughter."

"Can I say something?" Nancy still sat beside Allison, and her voice was tiny, but everyone stilled. "Mr. Dixon," she said, "you keep telling us that this play is all about fate, right?"

"Yes."

"So then Romeo wasn't really to blame for Tybalt's death." She paused, collecting her thoughts. "He was fortune's fool, right?"

"Oh, man," said Devin. He sat down with a thump.

"I think," Nancy began, "that according to the play itself, Fate was responsible. Romeo had no control over it. It was written in the stars."

Devin and Marc shook their heads in resignation.

"Case dismissed," I said.

———

The guidance counselor phoned me the next morning, before classes. The school board had special funding that year to hire a social worker, she said, someone who would focus on kids from immigrant families. She'd arranged for this person to come in, as well as the cultural liaison worker, and she asked if I could pop down and meet with them.

Kelly turned out to be a likeable ex-hippie from British Columbia and the liaison worker was Sayed, whom I'd worked with before during parent-teacher interviews. Sayed wore a stiff, slightly threadbare suit, but he carried himself with dignity. He was highly respected in his community. Kelly wore a loose, flowing dress and her hair, streaked with gray, was tied in a long ponytail that fell halfway down her back.

We met in the staff room. When I came in, they were waiting for me. "I have spoken with the father," Sayed started. "It is true. He has arranged a marriage for Sadia."

"But she's sixteen," I said.

"Seventeen, actually. Almost eighteen," said Kelly, thumbing through the file on the coffee table.

"But she's in grade ten," I said.

"Haven't you looked at this?" Kelly asked, turning over another paper. "She was kept back a grade, early on, so that she could learn English."

"She speaks perfect English, sometimes with a Scottish accent."

"She's had time to learn," Kelly said.

Sayed stepped in. "Her father knows she is a good daughter."

"Then, why the hell—" I began but stopped.

Kelly raised her eyebrows.

"The father allowed me to speak to Sadia," said Sayed. "She is very unhappy with this arranged marriage."

I took a deep breath. "Okay," I said, "so what can we do?"

"The father is a good man, this you must understand."

"Yes, but—"

"Perhaps if I speak with the imam at their mosque," said Sayed. "I know him quite well. I could ask him to speak with the father."

"That's good," I said. "Isn't it?"

"Another option is to rent Sadia an apartment," said Kelly, closing the file. There are funds for this kind of situation. She's almost eighteen. She can live on her own if she wants."

"She's just a kid," I said.

Kelly eyed me. "She's a very intelligent young woman. You said so yourself."

"Yes, I know. But that's a lot for her to—"

"I'm just telling you the options."

Sayed rubbed his chin. "Let me first speak with the imam."

———

A couple of days after I'd seen Rick and Claire on her back deck, Claire came over to watch some television. Outside, on my own back patio, a purple twilight hung above the trees. Claire seemed in good spirits. She lounged on my black leather couch and draped her legs casually across mine. On my flat-screen, the strident cello opening to *Game of Thrones* had just begun. The wheels and cogs of that imaginary world flickered across my living room.

"Glass of wine?" I offered.

Claire held up her hand to stop my pour. "Two ounces only," she insisted. I'd bought some Valpolicella from the fields outside of Verona, and I splashed it into her long-stemmed glass. She left it on the coffee table and leaned back. She loved *Game of Thrones*.

I considered telling her about the letter, but the show had already started and she was engrossed. She stretched out across the couch. I sipped at my wine, but I noticed that she didn't touch hers. Claire had to work the next day, and even before the end of the episode I could see her eyelids growing heavy.

"Enough?" I asked.

"Sure. Maybe we can leave the rest for later."

She untangled her legs and righted herself. She still hadn't touched her wine.

I walked with her to my front door and watched her slip on her shoes. She leaned in for a hug to say good night and that's when I felt it. Her stomach was as hard as a fist and I knew.

She was pregnant—Claire was pregnant—and I definitely wasn't the father.

I closed the door behind her, went back upstairs, and downed her glass of wine. I felt like I was plunging down in an elevator, that someone had just cut the cables, and there was nothing I could do to stop it.

About an hour later, I texted her. My hands were shaking. "I may be going crazy," I wrote, "but I have to ask: Are you pregnant?" I stopped for a moment, then added, "Is it Rick?" Rick, the renovations guy. I couldn't think of anyone else who it might be. She spent most of her time with me.

She texted back immediately and said, "No and NO." She used capital letters. And for a moment, I breathed a great sigh of relief.

She texted again. "Walk tomorrow?" she wrote.

"Okay," I tapped back. "How about in the morning?"

Claire and I had walked together hundreds of times over the years, but there was never to be a walk like this one. She was pensive when she came over, and we'd barely made it to the river, just a few hundred yards, when she said, "Okay, here's the thing. I *am* pregnant. I didn't want to tell you by text."

I couldn't breathe.

"You knew I had to go for some tests. I told you that."

She had told me. She had some medical appointments for something else entirely. I waited. She didn't make eye contact with me. Her eyes were fixed straight ahead. "I went in for the tests," she said, "but I came out with an unexpected result."

I barely heard half of what she said after that. My world was forever changed. Just like that. We walked almost to downtown and back, probably three hours. At some point, I asked, "It's Rick, right? The father?"

"No!" Claire said. "The father is not in the picture."

"Then . . . who?"

"Does it matter?"

"Of course it fucking matters."

"I'm sorry," she said.

"Jesus, Claire. I'm right here," I said. "I've always been right here beside you. For years."

She was near tears.

"I love you," I said. "Why didn't you ever . . . ?"

"I didn't want to wreck it. I didn't want to lose you. You said you didn't want kids."

"I didn't say that. I said it hadn't happened for me."

We walked on in silence and she cried quietly. "I'm sorry if I hurt you," she said after a while. She turned her wide green eyes on me. "Please," she said. "You are my best friend. I don't know what I'd do without you. Especially now."

She was plainly distraught, so I put my arm around her. Whatever I was going through, she was going through far worse. I knew that, even then. The simple fact is that she was going to have a baby.

I could have stepped up at that moment. I could have said that it didn't matter who the biological father was, that we were meant to be together. Now was the time to save her from her misfortune.

Only, life is not that simple. I'm going to be as honest as possible here. Maybe I could have become a sort of surrogate dad, but I'm not that young anymore, and that baby she was carrying wasn't mine. What's more, she never asked me to step in—not that I expected her to, not that she would have felt she had a right to ask either. And there was that insistent problem: that she would probably never see me as her lover, as her partner. All of this made me hesitate, as usual, until it was too late.

After dropping off Claire, I walked home, climbed upstairs, and saw the Italian grammar book in my office. I still had the damn letter from Juliet tucked away in it. Useless now, obviously. On the cover of the book was a harlequin plucking at a lute. In Italy this figure is known as Pulcinella—a cruel puppet wearing a beak-nosed Venetian mask and a black floppy hat. He creeped the hell out of me.

And he was leering at me like Fate itself.

———

"O, break, my heart!" *The fluorescent* classroom lights hummed above me. "These are Juliet's lines," I said. "In act 3, scene three."

Thirty pairs of eyes stared up at me. "It was Shakespeare who said it first. He invented that phrase."

Andy frowned. "But people were in love before Shakespeare, right?"

"Absolutely."

"Juliet's heart is broken?" Andy asked. He was thinking hard.

"Yes. She's—"

"But Romeo still loves her, right?"

"Yes, of course."

"So he's dumping her?"

"No, no. He's just murdered Juliet's cousin. It's kind of a problem."

There were nods around the classroom. They understood that much, at least.

"I want to talk today," I said, "about Juliet's soliloquy."

"Soliloquy?" said Devin.

"A soliloquy is when a character speaks his or her inner thoughts out loud to the audience. Usually, and especially in Shakespeare, it's a time for an actor to shine.

Like this. Listen:

Come gentle night . . .
Give me my Romeo; and when he shall die,
Take him and cut him out in little stars,
And he will make the face of heaven so fine
That all the world will be in love with night

"Is Romeo dying?" Andy asked. Allison, a few desks to the right, shook her head in the resigned fashion of one who is embarrassed by her boyfriend.

"In a manner of speaking," I said, "Romeo is already dead."

"Are you wrecking the ending?" Devin asked.

"You already know that they die, so no."

Only Minh looked a little startled by this revelation.

"Right from the beginning," I said, "Romeo and Juliet's fates were sealed. It was inevitable."

Allison shook her head sadly.

"No," I said.

A few heads rose.

"No," I said again, maybe a bit louder than I should have. "Fate," I pressed, "is just an illusion."

Andy glanced down at his book. "Mr. Dixon," he said, "where's that written?"

"It's not in the book," I said. "It's me, and I'm telling you that real life isn't a fairy tale."

"But—"

"Things are not preordained. Life is more chaotic than that. Everything seems fine, and then, *ka-boom*! The consequences of a thousand stupid decisions collide and blow your heart apart."

My students froze. Who was this person at the front of the room?

"Okay," I said. "Maybe that's enough for today. You can have free time till the bell rings."

When it did, they scurried out the door, no one daring to make eye contact with me. At the very end of the day, though, Marc appeared at my door.

"Mr. Dixon?" he said.

I glanced up from the papers I was marking.

"I just came by to say thank you."

Marc was a rough kid. Some of the teachers had already pegged him as a hoodlum. He smelled of pot sometimes. "Thank me for what?" I asked.

"For letting me be a part of your English class."

"You *are* a part of my class," I said.

He stood there a moment. "You know what I mean."

I looked at him now, this kid in his gangster pants, his eyes wide and vulnerable.

"Well," I said, "you're welcome."

He lingered at the door a moment longer. "And, I wanted to ask you . . ."

"Yes?"

"Is everything okay with you, sir?"

"I . . . uh . . . yes, everything's fine."

"Because you don't seem yourself these days."

He was right, of course, but I had no idea it was that obvious.

Marc shrugged like he was sorry for asking. "Okay, then," he said. "I gotta catch my bus."

"Right," I said. "Thanks for stopping by."

He lingered for another moment at the door, this tough kid, and I knew he understood.

6

Wilt thou be gone?

Outside the narrow classroom windows, the first bubbles of sap appeared on the poplar trees. Slender green shoots were breaking through the buds. The students tracked in mud from the melting fields and the sun rose high in a sky as blue as a robin's egg.

In the play, we'd come to the heart of it. We'd come to the scene that, for me, is much more poignant than the balcony scene. The lovers are in Juliet's bedroom. Romeo is lying beside Juliet just as the call of a lark drifts in through the window. They've been together the whole night, but now dawn is breaking and Romeo knows he must steal out of the city before sunrise or risk death. These are the lovers' last moments together. Only they don't know it yet.

Look love, what envious streaks
Do lace the severing clouds in yonder east.
Night's candles are burnt out, and jocund day
Stands tiptoe on the misty mountain tops.

I read the lines out loud to the class. "Did you understand all that?"

"Night's candles are the stars," Devin said.

"That's right," I said. "The stars are going out. Dawn is break-ing."

Andy put up his hand. "If the stars are going out," he said, "does that mean Romeo doesn't believe in fate anymore?"

I thought for a second. "Maybe."

Two rows over, Allison stole a glance at him. I think they'd been discussing this, maybe discussing my outburst the day before.

"*Oh thinkest we should ever meet again?*" I continued. "Juliet says this and there is no sadder line in all the play—because they won't. They will never be with each other again, at least not alive."

The clock on the wall ticked.

"Andy," I said, "do you want to read Romeo's answer?"

Andy shuffled in his seat, then read in a clear voice:

I doubt it not; and all these woes shall serve
For sweet discourses in our time to come.

Andy's eyes found mine, checking to see if he'd pronounced the words correctly. I gave him a nod.

"Romeo is saying that someday far in the future, they'll be able to laugh about all this."

"Only they won't," said Devin sullenly.

"No," I said. "They won't. It's over for them. It's over."

———

Claire fled for a couple of weeks. She went off to her family cabin, deep in the woods. She needed to escape for a while. I remember her shaking her head at the thought of it all. "It's real now," she said. "It's real."

My letter from Juliet was forgotten. The idea of taking Claire to Italy was dead. The days were lengthening and the evenings were growing warmer. Crocuses bloomed and the river swelled. Claire and I texted back and forth, meaningless pleasantries, and I really didn't know what was going to happen next.

Sometimes, in Shakespeare, you stumble across a line that speaks directly to you, a line that rings across the centuries and strains at your heart.

"*How is't, my soul?*" Romeo says to himself. "*Let's talk.*"

———

"*Okay,*" I said, "*where were we?*"

"Jeez, Mr. Dixon," Devin said. "Romeo's just gone out the window."

"Right, so then Juliet's mother comes in to tell her that she is to be married, immediately."

Devin and then Andy jolted in surprise. Allison raised her hand. "But Juliet's already married," she said. "To Romeo."

"That's the problem. No one knows that, though, and the father has arranged a marriage for her, a marriage she certainly doesn't want."

Sadia's desk at the front of class was still empty. And thank goodness. I'd been worried about going through this scene with her in the room.

"It gets worse," I said. "When Juliet's father bursts into the room, he goes completely insane because Juliet refuses to be wed. Then he attacks Juliet."

"Not cool," muttered Devin.

"Not cool at all." I read the father's lines. "*Hang, beg, starve, die in the streets for, by my soul, I'll never acknowledge thee.*"

"He'd leave her to starve in the streets?" Andy asked.

"Yes. At least that's what he says."

"But she's his daughter," said Allison.

"I know. He's on the verge of hitting poor Juliet," I went on. "She's crying, but her mother gets in front of Lord Capulet, the nursemaid does too, to protect Juliet from him."

"Whoa," said Devin. "This is crazy."

"Yeah, it is. At the very end, the father storms out and Juliet collapses on the floor in misery."

A pall hung over the classroom. "I think maybe that's enough for today," I said. "Maybe we can just watch a bit of the movie."

Allison nodded. "Good call."

———

After school, I spoke again with Sayed, the cultural liaison worker. "I have spoken again with the father," he said. His voice buzzed through my classroom phone. "I am sorry. He insists that he has made a good match for his daughter. I have also spoken with Sadia."

"Is she okay? She's missed quite a lot of school now."

"She is very upset."

"So what do we do?"

"You must understand, this is very difficult for everybody."

"Did you speak with the imam?"

"Yes. He also tried to reason with Sadia's father, but the man will not change his mind."

"Is he dangerous, do you think? The father?"

"Dangerous? No, no. It's not like the movies. He is a good man. He is quite traditional and he's trying to do his best for his daughter."

"Well, he's not."

"Maybe this is not for us to decide."

"It's for Sadia to decide," I said. "Isn't it?"

"Yes, with this I agree."

"So will you phone Kelly?"

I heard nothing but silence at the other end for a long few seconds. "Yes," he said. "Perhaps it is time to arrange an apartment for her—if this is what she wants."

By the end of the week, Sadia had moved out of her house. Kelly arranged everything. The principal got involved and so did the imam. I stepped back. Sadia's apartment was furnished with pots and pans and a TV and bedsheets scrounged from various teachers' homes. She had everything she needed to become self-sufficient.

———

The thing is, Sadia lasted exactly two nights in that apartment. She cried the whole time. She missed her family—including her father. Sayed phoned me on Monday morning—before classes started—to tell me all this. By that point, Sadia had packed up and gone back home.

That's not how this was supposed to turn out. We thought we were saving Sadia from a marriage she did not want. She herself had begged us to do so. I didn't really understand.

On the phone, Sayed waited for me to take it all in. "There's one more thing," he said, his voice calm on the other end of the line. "The father has decided to call off the marriage."

"What?" I said. "That . . . that's amazing." The time was eight o'clock. My students would be charging into class in about fifteen minutes. "What happened? Why the change of heart?"

"I believe the father realized that he would truly lose his daughter and he could not live with that. So," Sayed continued, "in the future, Sadia will be a part of any discussion about her availability for marriage."

"Okay," I said. "That's fantastic."

"I understand Sadia wants to go on to university," Sayed said.

"Definitely," I said. "She's one of my best students."

"They are, you understand, a very close family. And the father accepts her wishes to pursue an education."

"That's great," I said. "That's great news."

"Yes. As I said, her father is a good man and he has come to see the wisdom in this course of action."

As surprised as we all were by this turn of events, the research on love could have predicted this outcome. One of the most studied concepts in psychology is something called attachment theory. It goes back to one John Bowlby, who had some new ideas about human behavior in 1969. He rejected Freudian analysis and Pavlovian conditioning and wrote that we are literally hardwired to need human contact. Not just to want it, but to physically need it.

Infants need the caresses and swaddling of their mothers as much as they need food and shelter. And separation from their mothers is like a tiny death. In adult relationships, things are not so very different. We will go to extraordinary lengths to avoid the loss of love—all kinds of love.

Separation has two stages. The first stage is denial. A baby will wail its disapproval, but an adult may turn to drinking or other self-annihilating behaviors. The second stage is worse. It is a state of pure despair, more powerful and more sustained than almost any other human emotion. Of course, there's a neurochemical process underlying this—called the corticotrophin-releasing factor, or CRF for short—and yes it's the same paralyzing potion that hits junkies in withdrawal.

This might very well be the central problem of love. The aversion to loss is actually stronger—quite a lot stronger—than the rewards we feel when things are going well. We are, as I said, hardwired that way. It's a burst of neurochemicals that we are almost helpless to fight against. They are simply overwhelming.

Sadia was back in class the following day, but her eyes were red-rimmed. She moved self-consciously to her seat at the front and sat down without a word.

I waited a moment while the rest of the students settled. I tried to catch her eye, to silently welcome her back, but it was clear she didn't want to be singled out. She just wanted to be normal again.

"All right," I began, flipping open my book. "Romeo has fled. He's hiding in the nearby city of Mantua."

"And Juliet?" Allison asked. "What about Juliet?"

I stole another glance at Sadia. She didn't look up from her book, but she was listening.

"Juliet," I said, "goes to Friar Lawrence." I hesitated for just a second. "She says she's going to kill herself if he doesn't help her."

"And does he help her?" asked Allison.

"Yes, or at least he tries to. But get this," I went on. "Friar Lawrence says that she *should* kill herself."

"Good idea," Sadia grumbled.

"Whoa. What's with you?" Devin asked.

Sadia whirled on him. "What's with *you*?"

"Okay, okay," I said. "What's really happening here is that Friar Lawrence has come up with an idea. He thinks that Juliet should fake her own death."

I explained the Friar's expertise with herbs and plants, how he could concoct a potion to make her sleep for a time, to appear dead, then wake up some forty hours later. I waited for questions but there weren't any.

"So the plan is, Juliet will pretend to kill herself. Friar Lawrence will send a letter to Romeo explaining the plan, and then, when she does wake up, Romeo will be there and they can run off together. No one will ever know."

"Until they open the vault again," said Devin.

"Sure," I said, "but that could be months or even years later." I paused. "There's just one little problem."

It was Minh, quiet, diminutive Minh, who put up his hand.

"Minh?" I said. "You have something to say?"

"Star-crossed," he said. "They are star-crossed."

"Exactly," I said. "Nothing can stop what's going to happen next."

———

Claire texted me to say she would be returning the following day. But that didn't make sense. I was pretty sure Claire was already home. I couldn't help but notice that there were lights on at her house and that there was a truck parked in her driveway.

The next morning, I phoned her. "Hi," I said. "Welcome home."

"Thanks."

"Um, are you still doing renovations?" I couldn't get it out of my head, that truck parked in her driveway. It was obvious who it belonged to.

"Renovations? No, Rick just dropped by to say hi."

"Claire," I said, "c'mon, what's going on?"

"Okay." She sighed. "I'm coming over. We need to talk."

She appeared a while later, slinking around to the screen door on my back patio. The expression on her face was strained. We went inside and sat on my black leather couch. "You know most of everything," she said, "but there's one more thing."

My face tightened into a frozen smile.

"Rick *is* the father."

Even though I'd known it, hearing it confirmed was devastating. I was angry. I'd been blindsided—twice. "So now he's moving in with you? Is that it?"

No answer.

"You lied to me."

She wouldn't meet my eye. Outside, I could hear a train rumbling by.

"He came over one day," she said.

"Yeah?"

"He had come over to fix something or other—the hot water spigot, I think . . ."

"And . . . ?"

"I left the ultrasound pictures on the kitchen table." She glanced up then, meeting my gaze. Her eyes were liquid. "He saw the pictures and he knew."

I let out a single whimper of pain. I couldn't help it. I felt like I was underwater, that something heavy lay on my chest, pinning me down.

She spoke softly. "I told you—you can't help who you fall in love with."

I tried to say again that I had been right beside her all this time, all these years, that I had loved her, that that should count for something—but nothing came out. I raised my hands in frustration, then let them collapse on my lap.

Claire slumped on the couch, resting a hand on her belly. "It's going to be a boy," she said.

I folded over, elbows on my knees, my hands coming up to form a little triangle around my mouth. "I can't do this," I said.

"You were fine," she said, "with me being pregnant." I could see she was working up her argument. She'd always been good at that.

"You said the father wasn't in the picture."

"He wasn't then."

"I asked you point-blank if it was him. You lied."

"I was trying to protect him. He didn't even know."

"And now he's moving in?"

"I can't do this alone, Glenn."

"No," I said. The back of my jaw felt like someone was whacking it with a ball-peen hammer. "There's got to be another way. Please, I'm begging you. Don't do it like this."

"What am I supposed to do?" Her face contorted into agony. I knew she had very few choices. I knew this was hard for her, crushing for her, but I couldn't bear to have them living together and not so far away from me. I just couldn't bear it.

"Claire, I loved you . . ." I began again, but it was useless. "And now," I whispered, "I've lost you. I've lost you and it kills me."

When Claire left my place after that, I think we both knew it was for good. It would never be the same again. I hugged her at the door. In fact, we held each other for a while. I cupped the back of her head in my hand, felt her face buried into my shoulder. I'll never forget the look on her face when she drew back. She was as tortured and defeated as I was. And then, that was that. She whisked out the door and out of my life forever.

―――――

Devin came slamming into the classroom. "What happens next?" he demanded. Allison had opened her book. Andy was still settling into his desk. Sadia was pensive and quiet.

"Friar Lawrence," I said, "was supposed to send a letter to Romeo. He was supposed to tell Romeo about the plan. But his letter is never delivered." I flipped ahead a few pages.

Outside the classroom windows, the trees were coming into bloom. "The thing is," I said, "everything depended on that letter. Everything. And now, well, now things are . . ." My voice dropped away.

"Mr. Dixon?" asked Sadia. "Are you okay?"

I stared out over the rows of faces. "It's just . . . it's a tragedy," I managed. "It's all over for them. It's over."

"Mr. Dixon?" Sadia's eyes were wide.

I glanced at the clock. We had lots of time but I wanted to finish this scene. "And now," I said, "Romeo delivers what I think is one of the greatest lines in the play."

"You always say that," said Devin.

"*Is it even so . . .*" I began. I knew these lines by heart.

Devin grimaced, but he was listening, and I raised my voice, in spite of myself, and boomed out the line. "*Then I defy you, stars.*"

"Stars?" said Andy.

"Yes. You understand what that means? To '*defy the stars*'?"

Sadia's voice was soft, but it was dead quiet in the classroom. "Romeo's not going to take it anymore," she said. "He's going to fight against his fate."

———

That evening after school, I took the letter from Juliet out from Desiree's grammar book. I'd not been sleeping well or eating. I'd been a wraith for the last few days, and as I held that letter in my hands, I considered throwing it out or even burning it.

Desiree's book was flipped open to a map of Italy. Now, I don't want to say that it was a sign, exactly. I don't believe in those kinds of things, but there it was on the map, Verona, the city of Romeo and Juliet, circled twice in blue ink.

Desiree was back in Canada She lived for the winter months in Mexico, but she was home now, and I'd already e-mailed her to see if she'd pick up the damn book. I hadn't heard from her yet.

I needed to escape. I was falling apart, and as soon as the school year was over, I would get out as soon as possible. Rick had moved in and it was unbearable. But where would I go?

I thought again about the letters to Juliet, about my trip to Verona the summer before. I knew I hadn't really learned anything about love. All those broken hearts and it had come to this. Maybe, I thought, maybe I should just go back and try again. Dammit, maybe I wasn't finished with Juliet yet.

I made an appointment with the principal of the school, Mr. Tuff, and, yes, that was his real name. Everyone was a little leery of Mr. Tuff. All the teachers imagined you could wind up teaching Home Ec or something if you made a mistake. But I wasn't afraid of him. I was afraid of what I was about to do. I was about to quit teaching.

Oh, I was committed to finishing the school year all right—keeping myself busy till the end of June, but then I'd be gone. I've heard it called the geographic cure—running away to escape the pain, presumably as far away as possible. It wasn't quite as dramatic as faking my own death—but it wasn't so different, really.

I sat in the main office by Tina, the head secretary of the school. Along the glass wall of the school office was a row of chairs we called the Chairs of Shame. They were reserved for kids the teachers couldn't handle anymore, the ones sent to the principal's office. I slouched, and Tina pushed a bowl of candies toward me. "Looks like you need some," she said.

I grabbed a cinnamon heart and crunched down on it just as Mr. Tuff's office door creaked open. He ushered me in, over to an area he'd set up with a throw rug and a circular Formica table with a couple of blue chairs around it. He seemed to know that this meeting was going to require a more informal touch. His shirt collar was unbuttoned and he loosened his tie a notch. He heaved a sigh, closed the door behind me, and followed me over to the table.

"How long have you been teaching now, Glenn?" he asked.

"Twenty-one years."

He sat down on the chair beside me. "I've done thirty-seven."

"Thirty-seven. Wow."

Mr. Tuff stared at his bookshelf as if he were remembering all thirty-seven years. "You feel like you've paid your dues, Glenn?"

So he knew. I didn't even have to verbalize it. "It's not the kids," I said. "They're great. So are my colleagues."

"So?

"It's personal."

"You don't have to tell me." He leaned forward, interlacing his fingers. "Are you going to be okay?"

"Yeah, financially. But I just don't have the energy for teaching anymore."

"You have two months' vacation coming."

"It's not that. I just need to—"

"You need to make some big changes in your life."

"Exactly." I'd already completely muffed my rehearsed speech, but I felt I should give him a better explanation. "I'm think I'm going to go to Italy," I blurted.

"Italy? Didn't you go there last summer?"

"Yes. But now I'm going to go for longer."

"Do you speak Italian?"

"Not really."

His forehead creased. He probably thought I was making a mistake, but he wasn't going to say so. He leaned back and pulled a sheet from the shelf by his desk. "This is the form," he said. "It just requires a signature." He pushed it across the table to me. "You're sure about this?"

"Can I take this with me? Maybe think about it for a few days?"

"Of course," he said. He interlaced his fingers again. "In my experience," he said, "people don't regret making a change. When you decide you've had enough—it's probably because you have."

———

The sun warmed the planks of my back deck, and that's where I was sitting when Desiree came to pick up her grammar book. She swept in, tall and graceful. She'd been a ballerina. Her hair was long, a light brunette color with sun streaks of gold.

I must not have heard the doorbell, because she came around the back to find me slumped in a patio chair. She read my mood immediately and, without a word, she eased into the chair beside me.

"How did you make out with the Italian?" she asked. Desiree was the only person I knew who was actually fluent in Italian. The book was on the little patio table beside me.

"Not good."

"Something wrong?"

I hadn't told many people about Claire and the sudden turn of events. I was so completely defeated by it.

"I'm sorry to make you come over," I said. "I was going to give you your book back, but I think I might go back to Italy."

"Keep it then. It's no problem."

"I've kind of quit my job."

"Whoa. Okay." She leaned forward. "So what's going on?"

"It's a long story." I knew I needed to tell somebody, somebody who didn't know anything about the situation.

"I have some free time."

I took a deep breath. "Okay," I said. "There's this woman . . . I was in love with her for a long, long time but, well, it's all gone pretty crazy."

"Oh," said Desiree. "I'm sorry to hear that." She tipped her head and stifled a smile.

"What?" I said.

"I . . . I'm sorry, but I thought you were gay."

"What?"

"You dress well. You're nice and you're intelligent. And you're not already taken."

"And that makes me gay?"

"I just assumed . . . I don't know."

"I'm not gay."

"Well, all right. Good to know." She smiled again, and somehow that broke the ice.

For the next hour, I told Desiree everything. She remained silent through my story. I told her about Claire moving into a place not far from mine. I told her about Rick.

"You're kidding," she said. "That's crazy."

"Yes."

"Wow."

"Did you ever go to Verona when you lived in Italy?" I asked.

148

"I think so," she said. "Honestly, a lot of it blends together now. I lived in a bunch of different places in Italy."

"When was the last time you were there?"

"About ten years ago." She stared down at my deck.

"Don't you want to go back?"

"Of course I do." Her eyes met mine. "But I can't."

"Why not?"

"I left Italy," she said, "because of a guy."

My God, I thought. Everyone has a story.

Desiree clasped her hands behind her neck and leaned back in her chair. "His name was Rafael. We were together for five years. My longest relationship ever. We thought we were different from other couples. We thought the rules didn't apply to us. We thought we were safe."

"Safe? What do you mean?"

"In Italy," she said, "people are very superstitious. There's this superstition about accidentally brushing your feet with a broom."

"A broom?"

"It means you'll never marry. So Rafael and I used to brush a broom over our feet on purpose."

I sniggered.

"Yeah, well, clearly it didn't work. In the end, we got married."

"Wait, you're married?"

"I was, but I'm not anymore. That was a long time ago." Desiree looked away, across the grassy expanse that sloped down from my deck. "It's not what you think," she said. "Ever since I was a teenager, I wanted to live in Italy. Not just speak Italian. I wanted to *be* Italian— you know what I mean? I wanted to live there forever."

"Yeah," I said.

"I needed the marriage papers for my visa, so I could stay there. I begged him to marry me so I wouldn't have to leave. It was stupid."

Desiree sighed.

"We were together for four years before we were married. I loved him, but when we got married, well, things changed, and before the year was through we'd broken up. That was the end of us. I left Italy and I never went back."

Above the trees, the deep blue of the sky had faded to a soft, chalky pastel. In the east, a crescent moon, as pale as a scar, hung over the rooftops.

"Maybe you should come to Verona with me," I said. "Maybe you could answer some letters with me, improve your love karma."

"Are you serious—love karma?"

"It's just an idea. Maybe you could write your own letter to Juliet."

———

June is a strange time in the classroom. A long and magical summer lies just ahead for most students. The gym teachers were conducting their classes outside every day. My classroom windows were open and I could hear them out there, students running around, throwing Frisbees, barely supervised, as if they were practicing their freedom. We had only a few days of classes left. The exam schedule was posted on a bulletin board by the main office. Long rows of desks were being set up in the gymnasiums.

Just before the beginning of class, Andy came in with Allison. I was standing at the door, and I'd seen them come down the hall holding hands. She dropped his hand when she saw me. "Hey, Mr. Dixon," Andy said, breezing by me into the classroom.

The other students wandered in. Devin ambled through the door just before the bell rang. Sadia was already seated. She opened her text, flipping almost to the end.

"Okay," I said, "we're almost there. Just one more big scene."

"Finally," said Devin.

"Romeo," I began, "is going to sneak back into Verona."

They had all dropped their heads to read the lines, but Sadia's gaze remained on me. "To defy the stars," she said, almost under her breath.

"That's right," I said, "He's going back to Verona with poison to kill himself.

Juliet is about to wake up and Romeo has come into the church-yard. Friar Lawrence is on his way too—and it's just a matter of who gets there first."

"It's their fate," said Andy. He blinked at me and smiled.

"Romeo breaks into the vault and says, *A grave? Oh no, a lantern. For here lies Juliet, and her beauty makes this vault a feasting presence full of light.*"

"There's a light on inside?" Good old Andy.

"No," I said, "there's no light. It's a metaphor. Juliet is the light. Remember?"

Devin was looking at me in a strange way. "Mr. Dixon?"

"Yes?"

"Someone said you're not coming back next year."

All the students' heads sprang up.

"What?" said Allison.

"No way," said Andy.

Sadia's eyes had gone watery and wide. "You're leaving?"

———

I bought my ticket to Verona. I would have to fly overnight to London, cross up to Stansted airport and then fly to Milan. From there I would catch a train to Verona. I'd already written an e-mail to Giovanna asking if I could come and answer more letters. I don't know why I felt like a kid around her, as if I had just cracked a baseball through her kitchen window. But of course she said yes, she would be happy to have more help. Meanwhile, Desiree had sent me an e-mail. She wanted to know exactly when I was going to Italy. "As soon as I can," I wrote back. "As soon as the school year is over."

The end came, as endings often do, before I was really ready for it. We had one day left in the semester. The students were bouncing in with sunglasses on their heads, wearing board shorts and flip-flops. Some of the girls wore summer dresses. I had all the windows open and I'd already begun to pack my things into boxes.

My students nestled into their desks, the glow of summer on their faces. "Let's do the very end," I said. "Act 5, scene 3."

Sadia had her book open already. Everyone else was still finding their place.

"Romeo," I began, "sees that Juliet is dead."

"She's not dead," protested Allison.

"I know. I'm just saying—"

"She's *not* dead," Andy repeated.

"Yes, I know. But Romeo thinks she is. He's brought poison and he wants to lie down beside her and die."

Devin spoke. "That's so fucked up."

"Devin!" I stared him down. I wanted to give him a good scolding, but it was the last day.

"Sadia," I said. "Why don't you read Romeo's lines?"

"Romeo's?" she said. "But I'm a girl."

"So what?" I said. Truthfully, I wanted to hear her do her Scottish accent one last time.

O, here will I set up my everlasting rest,
And shake the yoke of inauspicious stars
From this world-wearied flesh.

"Stars," Andy said, as if it needed to be pointed out.

"To shake the yoke means to throw off what imprisons you, to break the chains of—"

"Fate," said Sadia.

"Yes, exactly."

She tucked her head back down to the text.

"*Thus with a kiss I die,*" I read, taking over from Sadia. I looked up from my text. "And he does," I said. "He drinks the poison and dies."

My students sat still in their desks.

"And just a fraction of a second later, Juliet begins to stir, first her fingertips, then her eyelids."

"Romeo dies?" Andy asked.

"Yes. He dies. He falls to the stone floor beside her. Juliet wakes to find him dead. She bends down and tries to kiss him—to taste any poison that might still be lingering on his lips. She wants to die with him."

The students were statues.

"She notices he has a dagger."

"Oh no," Allison whispered, her voice as soft as a brush on a chalkboard.

"And she stabs herself. In the heart. And all this, just a fraction of a second before Friar Lawrence comes rushing in."

"But it's too late," Devin said. "They're both dead."

Sadia glanced up at me, her eyes moist with tears.

I read the last lines:

A glooming peace this morning with it brings;
The sun, for sorrow, will not show his head.

For never was a story of more woe
Than this of Juliet and her Romeo.

I let it sink in, the finality of it. "And yet," I said, "there's sort of a happy ending."

Devin scowled. "Yeah, right."

Sadia too was unconvinced.

"Everyone forgets about it," I said. "Usually, the movies don't show this—but there's a hopeful ending."

"C'mon, Mr. Dixon," Devin said.

"What does it say at the very beginning of the play?" I asked.

"Oh no, Mr. Dixon. Let's not go back to the beginning. Not now."

"*A pair of star-crossed lovers take their life.*" I brought my voice down low. "*Whose misadventured piteous overthrow doth with their death bury their parents' strife.*" Thirty pairs of eyes locked on me, faces I would remember.

"Which means?" asked Devin.

"It means the fighting is over, the feud between the Capulets and Montagues. It's been going on for centuries. And now it's over. That's the point. That's what fate had planned all along. It was a catastrophe, but in the end, maybe it was the only way for the families to get beyond their petty squabbles. It was the only way to bring peace."

"Fate took away what was most important to both families: their children," said Sadia.

"Yes," I said. "And Lord Montague offers to build a statue of Juliet."

I recalled the bronze Juliet in the courtyard in Verona. It hadn't occurred to me until then exactly what it meant, how the statue fit with the hopeful end of the play.

Devin looked up at the clock. The bell was going to ring, my last school bell ever. "It's time, Mr. Dixon." He tugged his backpack up onto his lap.

"Yes," I said. "We're finished."

The students didn't hop up from their desks as I expected them to. Instead, they were whispering to each other. One or two glanced at me with mischievous smiles. Then all at once, they stood—the entire class—surrounding me. I still had my *Romeo and Juliet* text in my hands.

"Whoa," I said. "What gives?"

"Group hug!" someone called out. And they sandwiched me. Thirty of them. I didn't know what to say.

The bell rang, and my students bounded out the door. They were so young. Just beginning. They had no real sense of endings. They jumbled out the door, chattering and pushing, as if tomorrow morning they'd be in class again, as if they would always be this age, caught in perpetual youth, the whole world ahead of them.

On her way out, Sadia stopped and turned back. "Thank you, Mr. Dixon," she said. And then she too was gone.

Act Three

7

Any man that can write

Verona rained. It thundered and poured. I arrived on a dark and miserable evening and took a taxi to the *pensione* I'd booked online. The place wasn't far from the train station; in fact, it was in an apartment block tucked just behind the Franciscan monastery that housed Juliet's tomb.

A creaky old lift took me up to the third floor, and the owner, Emiliano, met me at the door. He didn't say much. He handed me a couple of toothy keys on an iron ring as big as a bracelet—one for the street entrance and another for his apartment. The front hall was lined with posters from classical music performances. A violin case sat on the floor beside the umbrella stand.

"You may choose one of the bedrooms at the back," Emiliano said, stepping aside to let me in. He'd divided the back rooms from the rest of the apartment with a sliding accordion door. "And please excuse me," he went on. "I am now practicing."

The door to his music room had a pane of wavy opaque glass. I watched him shuffle in, his distorted figure hunching down over a harp. The wood bracing of the harp curved over his head and he tinkled out a short baroque passage, a series of notes that chimed up and down a minor scale.

I chose the bedroom at the very back and heaved my bags in. I knew I should just climb into bed, but I was still wide awake, my circadian rhythms well out of sorts from the long flight. I sat by the bedroom window, which overlooked a tiny lane and a crumbling stone wall. Just behind the wall was Juliet's vault.

Okay, I thought. I've escaped. Now what? Here I was, back in Verona, a long way from my troubles, but I wasn't exactly feeling liberated. I was lost and alone on the far side of the world, and maybe I'd made a big mistake. I'd come thinking that I should write another letter to Juliet. Something a little more insistent. "Dear Juliet, what the fuck just happened to my life?" I pondered a few more choice phrases, but I knew that anger never helped anything.

Out front, Emiliano played on. The sound of the harp was soothing, a gentle plink of notes under the pattering of rain outside my window. I went to the washroom, toothbrush in hand, just as Emiliano finished his playing. We crossed paths in the hallway.

"*Buona sera,*" he said. "You cannot sleep?"

"*Buona sera,*" I said. "No, sorry. I heard you playing and, well . . . it sounded beautiful."

"Eh," he said, shrugging in resignation. "*Si può sempre migliorare.*"

"What's does that mean?"

"It means, 'One can always improve.'"

Yes, I thought, but how?

I did eventually fall asleep, and in the morning, the rain had let up enough for me to walk to the old office on the Via Galileo Galilei.

Raindrops plopped on my umbrella, but the worst of the storm was over. I stepped over puddles in the cobblestones and walked out across the dark bridge, down past the railroad tracks. At the entrance to number 3, I closed my umbrella and shook it out. Giovanna stood behind the reception counter with a sheaf of papers in her hand. "You have returned!" she said with a genuine smile.

"Yes, I—"

"You have come at a good time," she said, sidling out from behind the counter. "There have been some changes. You will have the same room, but . . ." Her heels clicked down the familiar hallway and I followed her. The office was considerably improved, furnished now with a shining hardwood desk and a proper office chair, padded in a plush blue fabric. The rough shelving along the wall was gone, replaced by an aluminum cabinet with sliding doors.

"I can't stay too long today," I said. "I arrived just last night. I'm—"

"Of course," she said, tipping her head. "Stay as long as you like."

I plunked myself down on the chair. "Is Anna coming in?"

Giovanna stood up a little straighter. "Anna will be working on some new ideas now." She paused as if unsure of something. "I will be at the front desk. Yes?"

The Gustav Klimt poster was still up on the wall. A battered cardboard box, bigger even than last year's, took up a good portion of the desktop. Outside, a dog barked and I reached for the first letter of the day. It seemed very strange to be back.

The letters were the same as ever—pleas, mostly from young women. *Where is my Romeo? How will I find him?* And my answers were rote. *Be patient. Your time will come.*

I worked for an hour or so, until I came to this one:

"Dear Juliet, I have come to spend the summer in Tuscany. I was in a relationship with a man named Jake who has played a significant part in my life for four years."

Four years. Exactly the time at which a lot of relationships fall apart.

"When we began," the letter went on, "we were madly, passion-ately, vibratingly in love. We spent all our free time together making beautiful memories. Then his father became ill. The sicker the father got, the more my love pushed me away. Then the man who wanted to spend forever with me cheated."

Bang. There it is.

"He continued on this destructive path for more than a year, treating me terribly and cheating behind my back. Destiny stepped in and I found out in an impossible, inconceivable way. I finally broke it off and spent a year wanting to hurt him until I grew sick of feeling anger all the time.

"We eventually got back together. Of course we did, but as won-derful as he now seemed to be, I could not let go of the past. I still held all of the hurt in my heart, and I realized there was so much more in this world for me. I realized I needed to find myself, and not myself in relation to him. So I broke things off and I have never felt such a wave of relief."

A dull ache gnawed at the back of my jaw. This letter struck a little too close to the bone.

This woman had felt relief, but where was mine? I'd escaped, all right, but there was no satisfaction in it and no cure. How long would that take? When would I ever feel happy again? It was all so unfair. I was miserable and lonely and the only difference now was that I was miserable and lonely many thousands of miles from home.

That night I went out to a restaurant that Giovanna had sug-gested. I found the Osteria al Duca up past the Piazza della Erbe. When I peeked in the window, the long benches were populated by locals. The room was rustic, with open beams across the roof and plank floorboards. A little plaque inside the door said that the build-ing dated back to medieval times and probably at one point had been the stables of the rulers of the city.

I sat by myself at the end of a long trestle table. The tables were

162

supposed to ensure that you wouldn't be eating by yourself. Eating is not a solitary affair in Italy. There's none of this business of wolfing down a meal in front of the television. Meals are a time for camaraderie, for family, a time to savor the company and the dishes. So I knew I was being a little out of line, sitting at the far end of the table, drawing my laptop out of my daypack and setting it up. I didn't care.

Giovanna had written down a couple of local dishes I should try. When the menu came, I settled on *bigole al torchio con ragù d'asino*. *Ragù*, I knew, meant a meat sauce served over pasta. The cathedral bells gonged six times—six o'clock then, very early for dinner by European standards.

Near the stairs leading up to the second floor, a woman sat at a tiny desk, squabbling into a phone. She didn't stop talking. She didn't seem to even take a breath. Her voice ripped through the room like a chain saw. She glared at me a few times, some poor sod in her restaurant, heartsick and alone, tapping at his computer. I put up my hand and she spat something more into the phone, put it down, and came over to me. *"Allora?"* she said, her hands on her hips.

I pointed at the ragù on the menu and she stomped off into the kitchen. About fifteen minutes later, she clattered my plate down in front of me.

"Grazie," I said meekly. She fluttered her hand and went back to her little desk. The dish looked like a nice spaghetti Bolognese. It tasted like spaghetti Bolognese too. I sprinkled real *parmigiano-reggiano* over it and tucked in. Only after trying it did I google *"ragù d'asino."* *Asino*, I learned, is the Italian word for donkey, coming from the Latin for "ass." Donkey meat, it turns out, is a local delicacy in Verona. I tried not to consider the maxim "You are what you eat," and I tried to avoid the proposition that the universe was trying to tell me something.

Okay, okay. Enough with the self-pity. I had to get it together. I'd told my students that *Romeo and Juliet* ended quite hopefully. It took a catastrophe for them to realize it, but the Capulets and Montagues had at last realized the futility of their centuries-old hatred. I'd suffered my own smaller catastrophe, but what epiphanies was I supposed to be drawing from all this? Love is a load of donkey balls, is that it? That kind of attitude didn't really get me anywhere. That didn't end the emptiness I was feeling, the hollowness in my gut, the tightness in my jaw. The best I could come up with was that I should just pretend to be happy. There's science behind that, but also a couple of thousand years of Buddhist philosophy. Just pretend to be happy and soon enough you actually will be happy.

I'd read before about brain plasticity. I knew that it was possible to rewire your brain by consciously changing your thought patterns. It's not easy, but it can be done. The initial research came from stroke victims who had managed to physically rebuild or rewire the damaged parts of their brains, sometimes beyond what conventional medicine had thought possible. Unlike any other organ in the body, the brain can reconstruct itself. It's a literal example of mind over matter.

So I could choose to be happy. I could choose to let things go and move on. It wouldn't be simple and it wouldn't be instantaneous, but choosing to do so would be the first step. The trick, I supposed, would be keeping up the ruse.

———

The next morning, I walked onto the bridge that led out of the Old City. I stopped for a while to watch the river heaving in dark slabs beneath me. Black clouds unfurled to the north over the Alps, and though the weather was trying to clear, it was still cold and gray. This wasn't anything like last summer.

I turned up my collar and scurried on, past the cemetery and down onto the Via Galilei. A gloom of warehouses and ugly apartment blocks lined the street, and every few feet spindly trees were optimistically planted alongside the crumbling concrete curb. There

wasn't any real sidewalk, just a pathway beaten in the wet grass beneath the trees. I plodded along, listening to the sound of my own
breath. Not a single car came by, not another soul.

I arrived at the meager parking lot and headed straight for the
front door. When I tipped it open, there, standing at the front, was
Anna. She had her boots on and was buttoning up her coat. She
glanced at me, but nothing registered. Then, "Glenn!" she cried. *"Ben
tornado!"* and she burst into one of her radiant smiles.

She lurched forward, kissing me on both cheeks. I bumbled
through this kissing thing, turning my left cheek first when it should
have been my right, but she just laughed. It was great to see her.

"I am on my way out. I'm going to meet Manuela," she said.
"We are talking about the tour now. I have some papers for her. You
remember the tour?"

"I remember," I said.

"And you still have your coat on," she said. "You must come. It is
decided."

Giovanna stood at the counter behind Anna. She'd only briefly
looked up when I'd opened the door, but then she'd gone back to
reading a paper that lay on the counter ledge.

"Is it okay?" I asked.

Giovanna nodded and returned to her reading, waving one hand
at us to flap us away.

Back out on Via Galilei I had to trot along to keep up with Anna.
The sky was spitting and she hoisted her umbrella. One spoke of it
kept poking me in the shoulder. "We are late," she said. "Manuela will
be waiting. She is very timely. How can you say this?"

"Punctual?"

"Yes. So much is happening," Anna said. "Here." She held her
umbrella higher and I ducked under it. "We are planning for Juliet's
birthday. You will be here on September 16?"

"Yes. I think so," I said.

"Good. You must attend. It will be nice." Anna cast me another of her smiles.

"I'm glad you have come back," she said.

And for the first time since arriving, I was glad to be back too. "Thanks," I said.

"Tell me, tell me, what has happened?" she said. "With your letter? With your love life?"

"Well," I said, "it's kind of a funny story."

Anna stopped and studied my face.

"Okay, maybe not so funny," I said.

She studied my face a moment longer. I think she knew I didn't want to talk about it. Not yet, at least.

"Okay," she said, "maybe we must hurry."

At the end of the bridge, we turned up a wide street, almost a square. Guardrails cordoned off an archeological dig in the subterranean gloom below the street level. I could make out contours of an old Roman road and the Ponte dei Leoni archway—the Gate of Lions. It once stood over the road that led to Bologna. There are no lions now, and it's just a blank wall that leads nowhere, the gate itself having been bricked in more than a thousand years ago.

We hurried by. Up ahead, I saw the familiar dovetail crenellations at the top of Romeo's house. "Are we meeting Manuela here?" I called after Anna, who had stepped ahead of me again. She didn't answer, but at the far end of the street, a woman turned. She wore a pea-green raincoat, sensibly enough, and she carried a yellow purse as big as a pillow. She moved forward and Anna passed her a file folder, which she dropped into her big purse. I'd reasoned that we'd be starting at Romeo's house, so I'd stopped there, just under the plaque that read THIS IS NOT ROMEO, HE'S SOME OTHER WHERE. But Anna turned and waved at me to join them at the end of the road.

"Glenn," Anna said when I caught up, "this is Manuela. Manuela, may I present Glenn. He is an expert on Shakespeare."

"Well, I don't know if I'd say expert."

"Piacere," said Manuela, dipping her head slightly.

"He has seen the first book of *Romeo and Juliet*," said Anna, "in, where did you say?"

"In the British Library."

Manuela studied me. She had a kindly face. She was older and very much shorter than Anna. "We are thinking of beginning the tour here," she said. She spoke with a classic Italian accent—an up-turned *a* on the end of almost every English word. "It is-a the important-a history," she said, touching her hand to the wrought iron fence that rose up beside us.

"You're not starting at Romeo's house?" I asked.

"No," said Manuela. "We will start with the true history. If you look here . . ." She tapped at the elaborate ironwork again. It enclosed a courtyard and the Santa Maria Antica church. "Do you see?" Manuela asked.

I didn't know what she was talking about.

"Here," she said. "This is the insignia of the Scala family." Wrought into the fencing were what looked like tiny iron ladders.

"Ladders?" I said.

"Stairs," she said. "*Scala* means 'stairs.' And behind this . . ." In the courtyard were four or five massive tombs, like Gothic gazebos, intricately carved from white Carrara marble. One tomb towered ostentatiously above the rest, a stone sepulcher as elegant as a cathedral spire, with a life-size equestrian statue on top. "That one," said Manuela, "is the tomb of Cangrande della Scala."

"Della Scala?"

"In Shakespeare, the name is Escalus."

"Like, Prince Escalus?"

Manuela smiled. "Of course."

"Are you saying Prince Escalus was a real person?"

"Yes. That is his grave. Right there."

"What?"

"He was the ruler of Verona in 1302, the year in which Romeo and Juliet's romance occurred. Prince Scala told the story to Dante."

"Wait," I said, shaking my head. "Like Dante Dante?"

"Yes. Dante Alighieri wrote much of his *Divina Commedia* here in Verona. You did not know?"

"No, I didn't."

Manuela *tsk*-ed at me. "Dante wrote the names in his *Purgatorio*, Capulet and Montague."

"Are you kidding me?"

"In 1302, yes. It was the time when the two families were fighting. This is certain."

"But . . . that's amazing. You're telling me it's a true story—a daughter from one family and a son from the other, falling in love? Here, in Verona?"

"Yes." Manuela flipped her wrist over and checked her watch. "We cannot know for 100 percent, but we believe it is a true story." She turned back to Anna, who'd been quiet all along, a bemused expression on her face. "*Grazie,* Anna," Manuela said, tapping at her big yellow purse and the papers inside. "You must excuse me now," she said. "I must go to meet my daughter. But Glenn—she turned her gaze on me once more—"you should look in Dante. *Purgatorio*. Canto 6, lines 106 to 108. There, you will find it."

"Canto 6," I mumbled, trying to commit the lines to memory. "One-oh-six to one-oh-eight. Yes, I'll look."

Manuela tipped her head once more. "Then you will understand," she said. "Juliet was real."

When Manuela left, Anna and I walked to the new office on Vicolo Santa Cecilia. We tracked wet footprints up the marble steps and slopped across the foyer to the glassed-in office. It was dark, and when she flipped the light switch, there was a loud pop and a fizzle of electricity.

"*Che palle,*" Anna said, under her breath. She put her hands together in a sort of prayer of frustration; then she plunged into the shadows and hoisted a small desk lamp from the corner. She pulled the lamp over to the wooden table in the middle of the room and switched it on. The lamp cast a pale yellow swath over the pile of letters there, unsorted, a swamp of colors and envelopes.

"We are having a problem with the lights," Anna said. "With the electricity."

"It's okay," I said. "I like this better anyway."

"It is the correct mood," she said.

"Yes, it's more atmospheric."

The dim yellow light washed across the ancient stone walls, almost like candlelight, and I remembered that this had once been a goldsmith's shop hundreds of years ago. Anna pulled out a chair and I sat beside her. She reached for an envelope, but she didn't open it.

"How's everything going with you?" I asked. I could tell by her eyes that her attention was not on the letters.

"It is not the best," she admitted. "Maybe I am almost finished with the Club di Guilietta."

"Anna? Why?"

"It is nothing." She forced a smile of resignation. "I need to find a career path for myself." She touched the corner of her glasses with two fingers and gazed absently at the envelope still in her hand. "I have been giving all my time to the club, but it is time for me to start . . ." She shook her head. "To start my life." She paused. "But what about you?" she said. "What has happened with your letter? Will you tell me now?"

"I got an answer," I said. "But by the time I did, it was too late and, I don't know, I didn't really act on it."

"She is gone?"

"She got pregnant, and it wasn't mine."

Anna raised her eyes to study me. "I am very sorry."

"It's okay," I said, trying to brighten. "I'm back. I'm going to answer more letters. I'm going to figure everything out."

She nodded once, almost to herself, and pulled the letter from the envelope. "Probably we should start then."

I pulled an envelope in toward me. I read it, but it wasn't really registering. There was more on my mind.

"Anna," I said, "can I ask you something?"

The light from the lamp made a halo around the tips of her hair.

"What would you say *you* have learned from all these letters? What are we supposed to be getting out of all this?"

She sighed and brought her letter up, holding it to her heart. "I think every time you answer a letter, you answer yourself also."

"I guess so," I said.

"And from every letter," she went on, "you can learn to be a better person, to imagine what you might do in that situation."

"It's like practicing," I said, "to try and improve."

"It is true." Anna lay her letter back down on the table. "I have learned that the people of the world are all the same. My problems are only small ones." Her voice was soft, almost a whisper. "I had many ideas for the club, but the economics are not good right now. Italy . . . it is a difficult time for us."

Then she smiled, hesitantly at first and then radiantly. "The lights," she said, gesturing at the darkness around us. "Not even the lights can work properly."

———

It was late when I finally got back to Emiliano's. I ignored the creaky old lift. It was just as fast to walk up the three flights of stairs. I pushed the comically large key into the lock and clicked the door open. All was dark inside when I plodded across the wooden floor to my room at the back. I was wide awake, still a little ragged from my escape, but Verona was beginning to work its magic. I felt, for the first time since

I arrived, something like tranquility. I pulled out my laptop to check for the day's e-mails. The screen flickered into being—a blue constellation of stars, a whirling galaxy—and I clicked open my mail server. At the top was a message from Desiree.

"I'm coming to Italy," she wrote. "I'm flying into Milan on Thursday."

It was already Tuesday. I thought for a moment and typed back: "I'm in Verona. You should come and visit. Maybe you should answer some letters with me. Do you want me to ask Giovanna if it's all right?"

Desiree must have been sitting at her computer at that moment, because the reply came almost immediately.

"Yes, and yes," she wrote.

For a moment, I regretted it. I hardly knew her. On the other hand, she was fluent in Italian and that might be good. And maybe it would be fun to have someone else to travel with, someone to laugh at my jokes.

She arrived two days later, in the afternoon. I met her at the train station. A wheel had cracked on her suitcase. It careened and bounced behind her, but she strode gracefully over to where I stood waiting.

"You made it," I said. I made a move to hug her, but she was distracted and pulled away.

"Are you okay?" I asked.

"I don't know about this." She gazed past me, searching. The train station was not about to win any awards for architectural beauty, but it seemed she was transfixed by it. "I was worried," she said, "that I might run into trouble at immigration."

"But everything's okay?"

"Yes," she said. "But now this stupid suitcase is broken."

"Maybe we can get it fixed. Here, I can take it." I motioned at the suitcase and she turned it over to me. She worked up a smile for me.

"Everything is all set," I said. "Emiliano has an extra bedroom and his place isn't far from here."

"Okay," she said. Her features were strained, her mouth tight and grim.

I stopped. "Are you sure everything's all right?"

She shook her head and I put a hand on her arm.

"It's going to be fun," I said. "C'mon. You'll see. You'll like it here."

Her fingers fumbled to the little locket around her neck. "You're right. I am glad I came. I needed to do this." She nodded and seemed to look around for the first time. "I can't believe I'm back in Italy."

Outside, the sky was clear for the first time in days. "Let's get a taxi," I suggested. I yanked on the suitcase. It lurched and almost fell over and she laughed for the first time.

Honestly, I wasn't sure about this either. I liked Desiree well enough, but I was worried that it might be kind of weird. We hadn't really planned this trip. It had just sort of happened.

A white taxi pulled up and the driver jumped out and popped open the trunk.

"*Buon giorno,*" I began, hauling Desiree's suitcase forward. The driver heaved it into the trunk and I dug in my pocket for a scrap of paper with the address. "Number 7, Via dei Montecchi," I said. The taxi driver glared at me without comprehension.

"*Fammi vedere,*" Desiree said, pulling my hand and the scrap of paper up to scan it. "*Quanto ci fa pagare per andare a Via dei Montecchi?*" she asked. "*Numero sette?*"

The taxi driver nodded. "*Dieci euro.*"

"*Va bene,*" said Desiree. Then she turned to me. "It'll be ten euros."

In less than ten minutes, we were at Emiliano's. I paid the driver and hoisted Desiree's broken suitcase out of the trunk while she spoke some more with the driver. He waved merrily at her as he pulled away from the curb.

She was staring up at the building now. It was hard to read her thoughts. Was she tired? Or was she wondering if she'd made a mistake? I maneuvered her suitcase into the dark foyer. "We can take the elevator," I said. We shuffled into the lift and I clanked the iron grating shut. It clattered up slowly and there was an almost uncomfortable silence between us.

"I hate elevators," Desiree said. The lift was not much larger than a closet, and we were pushed in awkwardly close together.

"Are you claustrophobic?"

"I was stuck in one once. The motion makes me feel barfy," she said.

She had been on two planes, a train, a taxi, and now a creaking, coffin-like lift. That was enough for anybody.

"Do you want to sleep or head to the office before it closes?"

"I'd just as soon get started. I want to meet Giovanna."

I opened the door to the flat. Emiliano was nowhere to be seen, and the front room was empty. Off to one side was a long table where Emiliano usually set out the breakfast things. Under a glass cover sat a cake. Emiliano must have baked it that morning.

"Pan di spagna!" cried Desiree, crossing the room. She lifted the cover and inhaled deeply. "Oh, I love this." A golden light slanted in from the windows. It caught her cheek and her soft jawline. It all looked like a Renaissance painting.

"I'm glad you came," I said.

Her eyes caught mine, two blue planets. "I'm glad you asked me," she replied. She lifted a small paring knife that sat beside the cake. "What do you think? Should we have some cake before we go?"

"Is it good?" I moved closer.

"This is Italy," she said. "Of course it's good."

Half an hour later, we were walking along the river. The sky had clouded over again. Up ahead were the church spires and red-tiled roofs of the Old City. "Just up there," I began, "is the Roman arena. It's the third biggest in the world, but you can't really see it from here."

I felt like a hack as a tourist guide. She'd grown quiet again. We crossed the bridge and veered right, past the cemetery, past the train tracks, down into the industrial ghettos of the city.

"Where exactly is this place?" Desiree said.

"Not much farther."

Desiree soldiered on beside me, stepping around the puddles from the rain the day before. "I should have brought my boots," she said.

"Boots?"

"It's cold. My feet are cold. My mom told me to pack light, so I left my boots behind at the last moment." She sighed.

"It's not much farther."

"I don't know about this."

Down the road, I could see the entrance to number 3. "It's right there," I said.

"Are you sure this is going to be okay?"

"Of course. Why wouldn't it be?"

"I'm probably not the best person to be doling out love advice."

"I wasn't either when I started. You'll be fine."

"And I barely know *Romeo and Juliet*. We didn't study that one in school. We did the one with the witches."

"*Macbeth*," I said.

A wall to the side of the front door had been wallpapered with fake bricks and a scatter of old letters were tacked onto it. Desiree studied one of the letters and frowned. "I don't know," she said. "Maybe I'm not cut out for this."

I swung the door open, and in the darkness Giovanna stood behind the counter. Desiree shuffled in behind me.

"*Buon giorno*," I said, and Giovanna nodded.

"Giovanna," I said, "this is Desiree, who I told you about."

"Of course," Giovanna said. "It is lovely to meet you. We have everything ready." She stepped out from behind the counter and breezed smartly toward us.

"*Buona sera*," Desiree said. "Thank you for having me."

"This is your first time to Verona?" said Giovanna.

"No, I lived in Italy. A long time ago."

"*Allora, parli italiano?*"

"*Sì,*" said Desiree. "*Ho vissuto in Italia per otto anni.*"

Giovanna's face brightened. They chatted awhile and I stood behind them, smiling awkwardly until their conversation petered out and Giovanna invited us to the small office at the back. I sidled in, pulling an extra chair to the desk so that Desiree and I could work together.

"Is there anything you will need?" asked Giovanna.

"No, no," I said. "I think we're fine."

"*Va bene,*" she said. She smiled once more at Desiree, then turned to leave, her heels clicking down the hallway back to her counter.

"She's really nice," Desiree said.

The cardboard box of letters sat heavy on the desk. "What were you two talking about?"

"Oh, I just told her about my studies at university. She studied languages too in Bologna, and international relations, just like me."

"She never asked me what I studied."

"She said you would show me what to do with the letters."

"I will," I said. I plucked a letter from the top of the box. "It's not that hard."

"There are an awful lot of letters," she said. The box loomed in front of us, brimming, overflowing. "You have to take them one at a time." I slid a letter out of the first envelope.

"Dear Juliet," I read out loud. "There's a boy back home. I don't know if he likes me, but I really love him. There's another boy, Jason, who is more interested in me. He is always looking at me, but I don't like him as much."

"That's it?" Desiree asked.

"Lots of them are like that, I'm afraid. They're young. They think they're in love."

"So what are we supposed to say?"

175

"Mostly you reiterate what they've written. Say something hopeful, and then you can sign it 'Juliet,' though I usually sign as 'Juliet's secretary.'"

"Because you're a guy?"

"Yeah. And then you tuck your answer in one of these envelopes over here, but don't seal it. Someone else will put the return address on it."

"Okay," she said. "But that still doesn't tell me what I'm supposed to say. I mean, what about this girl, this . . ." she looked at the name. "Andrea?"

"You have to be encouraging. Just reassure her that she's okay."

"What would you write?"

I picked up the pen and started. "Dear Andrea. Thank you for your letter." I stopped and tapped the pen on my lips.

Desiree was staring at me like I was an idiot. "And . . . ?"

"Just let me think for a second."

"How about this? May I?" Desiree took the pen from me and started on a new piece of paper.

Dear Andrea,

Thank you for your letter. Only you can know what's best for you. Listen to your heart and it will guide you.

"Sure," I said. "That's pretty good."

Desiree was already writing again. "The other boy, Jason, seems genuinely interested in you, maybe for who you really are, and that's important. You must always take care of yourself first. You must ask yourself what you really want."

It was a good answer, I had to admit. It made me think about what I really wanted. Did I know? Maybe just someone who would understand me. Someone who would care about me.

"So what do you think?" asked Desiree.

"Pretty good, you know, for a first time."

"What was that Shakespeare quote you said you used all the time?"

"To thine own self be true?"

"Perfect," said Desiree, and she closed off the letter with that.

We didn't stay long that first day. When we left, a patch of blue sky had opened up in the east. The sun was peeking through and we decided to walk into the Old City.

"Is there a moat?" Desiree asked as we crossed over the bridge. "I remember seeing a moat when I was here."

"I don't think so."

The medieval city walls reared up on our left. To our right, a wide piazza opened. In the middle of it rose the Roman coliseum, still far in the distance. "Do you remember that?" I said.

"Not really." We edged across the piazza toward it. A fenced-off section held one of the massive props they'd used in the *Romeo and Juliet* opera. A little farther on, a pair of Egyptian heads, King Tut masks at least ten feet tall, stared down at us.

"What are those?" she asked.

"Props for the opera," I said. "Those ones look like they're for *Aida*."

"Maybe we could go sometime," she said.

"Maybe." We walked on in awkward silence. Eventually, we passed under a Roman Gate—the Porta Borsari—which had once been the main entrance to the city.

"I really don't remember any of this," Desiree said.

"Were you here with . . . him?"

"No. I came with some friends. We came for Sunday brunch. *La Buona Domenica* is a big deal in Italy."

Up ahead, the rusty red bricks of the Castelvecchio—the old castle—appeared. The towers and ramparts jutted up into the evening sky. A tour bus chugged by, all the heads turned away from us, gaping at the fortress.

"This," I said, "was the castle of the Cangrande."

"The big dog?"

"Yeah," I said. "Cangrande was the prince—as in Prince Escalus."

"From *Romeo and Juliet*?" she asked.

"Yeah," I said. "Come on, I want to show you something." I took her arm, and we crossed the street to the other side, where a narrow passageway opened up in the castle walls. "Through here."

The stones under our feet were worn, centuries old. I kept my hand on her forearm for a few more steps and we strode up an incline. Along the tops of the walls were the same swallowtail crenellations I'd seen on the top of Romeo's house. A busker playing an accordion sat on a ledge. The sun was sinking over the walls.

"Is this part of the castle?" Desiree asked.

"Yeah, we're actually out on a bridge. You can climb up there onto the ramparts and look out over the river."

"Hmmm," she said.

"What?"

"Well," she said, "it's a good metaphor don't you think? We're crossing a bridge but you can't even tell it's a bridge."

"Ha," I said. "I'm usually the one boring my students with metaphors."

She glanced sidelong at me.

"But that's a pretty good one," I admitted.

We stopped near the busker and listened for a while, but I could tell she was fading.

"You getting tired?" I asked.

"Are you?"

"Yeah. I think I'm about done."

We doubled back and just before we came out onto the street again, Desiree stopped. At a gap in the wall, far below, the ground dropped away into a deep trench.

"Hey," she said, grabbing at my arm. "Look down there."

"In fair Verona, where we lay our scene." Thanks to Shakespeare's choice of setting for his famous star-crossed tale, this small Italian city is known worldwide as the home of romance, destiny, and true love.

The facade of Juliet's house. The house itself is seven hundred years old and belonged to the Cappelli family—rewritten as Capulet in Shakespeare's version of *Romeo and Juliet*.

Juliet's letter box in the courtyard of her house.

Juliet's balcony, really a Roman sarcophagus attached to the house in the late 1930s.

The statue of Juliet—note how her right breast is polished to a sheen by her thousands of admirers.

Giovanna Tamassia now manages the day-to-day activities and funding of the Club di Giulietta. She is also the daughter of the club's founder, Giulio Tamassia.

Giulio Tamassia first established the Club di Giulietta as an informal gathering of friends who discussed love, life, and politics. It was more than a decade later when the club became associated with Juliet's secretaries.

Just some of the many letters scattered across my desk during my time as a secretary to Juliet.

Anna working in her office at the Club di Giulietta.

On the walls of Juliet's house, the faithful plaster their messages using everything from bubblegum to Band-Aids.

On the top floor of Juliet's house, these stars are painted onto the ancient roof, providing the metaphor for Shakespeare's star-crossed lovers.

Soňa and me collecting the letters from the letter box in the courtyard of Juliet's house.

At the ancient Roman coliseum in the center of Verona, twenty thousand people watch the operas that are presented every night during the summer.

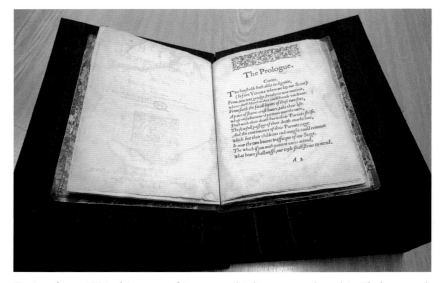

Dating from 1599, this copy of *Romeo and Juliet* was produced in Shakespeare's own lifetime, only a few years after he wrote it. It's currently held in the vaults at the British Library in London, England.

The vault and sarcophagus said to be Juliet's grave.

Working away at the endless letters on my second trip to Verona.

Desiree Bilon

The red bricks of the Castelvecchio, or old castle, with its fortified bridge.

Manuela, one of the secretaries, is interviewed by Jolyon Jenkins from the BBC.

The podium where we read our letters during Juliet's birthday celebration. Behind it is the beautiful staircase that leads up to the Lamberti Tower.

Desiree making last-minute edits on the letters we read aloud at Juliet's birthday celebrations.

Giovanna and her father, Giulio, at the celebration of Juliet's birthday.

Desiree and me, on top of the Scala di Ragione, just after Juliet's birthday celebrations. She's wearing the locket inscribed inside with "to thine own self be true."

Desiree and me on a beach in our tropical paradise, one year after leaving Verona.

Beneath the redbrick walls, half-hidden in the shadows, was the moat, dry now, probably dry for hundreds of years.

"I knew there was a moat here," she said. "I knew it."

"Is that another metaphor?" I asked.

"Hey, you just smarten it up, mister." She turned on me then, but she was grinning, enjoying herself. "Sometimes," she said, "you see what you want to see."

———

That night, the wrought iron streetlights lit up like stars. Old men lounged on their balconies and smoked. We came in from dinner, a pizza place we'd found under the medieval walls, and Desiree headed straight for her room. "Good night," she said, not turning around. "I'll see you in the morning."

"Good night," I answered, and I went to sit by myself in the front room. I pulled out my notebook. I wanted to write another letter to Juliet. I wanted to get it right this time. "Dear Juliet," I began, "I have come again to Verona with a shattered heart. Sometimes, I think, it is best to just flee—to put some distance between yourself and the sharp edges of fate. The girl I loved for many years did not love me. I despair of love, Juliet. I have been hurt many times and I am worn out and cynical. I am afraid of growing old alone. It's too much. I think I am a good person, and I don't know why this keeps happening to me."

I stopped. I didn't know what else to write and it just sounded like whining anyway. I heard the accordion door ratchet open and Desiree's footsteps tapping down the hallway. She drooped in toward me, her laptop tucked under her arm. "I can't sleep," she said.

"Me neither."

"What are you doing?"

"Writing another letter. The first one didn't work out so well."

She yawned and sat down beside me. She popped open her

laptop and it cast a bluish light across the tabletop. She'd changed into pajamas—flannel boxer shorts and a tank top—and her hair was up in a ponytail.

"Hey," I said, "could you look something up for me?"

Her eyes flickered over to me. "What?"

"Dante," I said. "*The Divine Comedy.*"

"What for?"

"I just want to see something. Canto 6 in *Purgatorio.*"

She tapped at the keyboard and a page opened up.

"Lines 106 to 108."

"Okay," she said, scrolling, squinting at the screen. "Here it is."

I leaned in to read it.

Vieni a veder Montecchi e Cappelletti
Monaldi e Filippeschi, uom sanza cura
color già tristi, e questi con sospetti

"Can you translate that for me?"

"Come and see," she said, "Montecchi and Cappelletti."

"Wow," I said. "That's them. That's the two families—Montague and Capulet."

She traced her finger under the second line. "There are two more names, then '*uom sanza cura.*' That means 'men without cure.'"

"Without cure?"

"I think it means something like without hope, without the possibility of release. This is Purgatory, remember."

I shuffled in a little closer to her. Her hair had a faint fragrance—and her bare shoulder touched mine. It was as soft and smooth as caramel.

"The last line is . . ." She squinted into the computer. "Already sad, these with suspect."

"Suspect?" I said.

"That's just the rhyme," she said. "He uses *sospetti* to rhyme with *Cappelletti.*"

"I don't get it."

"They're in Purgatory," she said again. "They've done something awful, but maybe something for which they can still make amends."

"Their hatred led to the suicides of their children, but it also brought peace to two warring families."

"That makes sense," said Desiree.

"Manuela told me that Prince Escalus told this story to Dante, that it actually happened in Verona just before Dante arrived. That was three hundred years before Shakespeare."

"Do you think it could be true?" Desiree asked.

"Juliet's house really is the Cappelli family home. Romeo's house is fake, but Manuela said there probably was a Montecchi family who lived just outside the Old City walls." I stopped. A chill ran down the back of my neck.

"Via dei Montecchi," she went on. Her eyes were as wide as mine. "We're right on the Via dei Montecchi, and we're south of the medieval walls."

"Holy shit," I said.

"Maybe," she said, "maybe, Romeo lived right here."

Arise, fair sun

esiree was up before me, already sitting at the breakfast table when I plodded into the front room. I'd stayed up late doing more research on the real Romeo and Juliet story, and I'd come across a few more tantalizing clues. The early-morning light washed across the plank flooring. Desiree's long hair shone, tipped in gold. *"Buon giorno,"* she said. "Did you have a good sleep?"

"Pretty good, yeah. How about you?"

"Weird dreams," she said. "But good."

On the side counter, Emiliano had set out granola, orange juice, cheese, and yogurt. Half the *pan di spagna* was still there under its glass bell. I took a yogurt cup and sat down beside Desiree.

A pretty little locket dangled from her neck. I'd noticed it from the beginning—rectangular, like a tiny illuminated book from the

Middle Ages, with fine lines of filigreed silver tracing across its cover.

"Does that open?" I asked.

"This?" said Desiree, touching the locket. "Yes." She plucked at it and a tiny hinge swung wide. It was empty.

"It's beautiful," I said.

"Thank you. My mother gave it to me."

"You should put something in it."

"I know. I will, when I find something I like."

"Listen," I said, "I was thinking maybe we could visit Juliet's vault before we go into the office. It's right behind this apartment block."

"Isn't that a bit creepy?"

"Kind of. But seriously, it's right there." I pointed at the wall to the back of us.

After breakfast, we gathered our things and tramped down the stairs together. We walked along the rain-spattered sidewalk to the end of the block and then up a lane and into the old abbey ruins.

"You brought your camera, right?" Desiree had an expensive camera, a Canon 5D Mark III, and she was just getting into filmmaking. She patted her daypack. It weighed heavily on her shoulder.

We crossed a grassy quadrangle, what used to be the cloisters of the old abbey. In the center was an ancient well, like a wishing well. Past it grew an oak tree, skeletal and ancient. All this was once hallowed ground. For centuries it had been a monastery, then a convent, then an abbey.

"The vault is down here," I said.

Desiree wrestled the camera out of her pack and snapped a photo of the wishing well. Her eyes narrowed at the steps. "I don't know about this," she said.

"Come on. It's not that bad."

I went first. The stairwell smelled like wine that had gone off. Desiree trailed behind me and our footsteps echoed in the silence.

The first cavern had tombs set into the floor, unmarked with dates or names, and Desiree bent to her camera again. She twisted at the lens. "It's a bit too dark in here," she said but clicked off a shot anyway.

"I was reading about this place last night," I said as she worked. "There's a reference to it from the fifteen hundreds."

"Mm," she said, focusing.

"The sarcophagus was used as a water trough up by the cloisters."

Desiree peered up from her camera viewfinder. "Which one is hers?"

"Juliet's tomb is in the next room."

I stepped ahead of her. The cavern was the same as last year, probably the same as it had been for centuries. A barrel vault of dusty bricks, like an ancient wine cellar, arched above us and in the middle of the floor an unadorned stone sarcophagus sat there like a bathtub. At the end of the cavern were two Venetian arches set in a niche.

"What the historian said was—"

"What historian?" She brought the camera up to her eye again.

"A historian from 1540 or something. He wrote that this sarcophagus originally had human bones in it but the people threw them out and set it up as a water trough."

"You love that history stuff, don't you?"

"It's interesting," I said.

She lowered her camera. "I like that about you, that you're always curious."

Desiree steadied herself and snapped another shot. Her flash went off and the sarcophagus shone for a moment, the shadows black and deep around it.

"So what about Juliet's bones?" she said. "Do you really think they were thrown away? Italians are very respectful. I can't believe they'd just—"

"That's just the point," I said. "For the bones to be tossed out like that, this historian figured they had to be the bones of a person who'd committed suicide. They wouldn't have been treated with respect."

"A suicide?" she said.

"Well, yeah. First of all, the sarcophagus was buried outside the actual cemetery, so it almost certainly held the remains of someone who had committed suicide. Suicide was considered a mortal sin, so the body couldn't be buried in hallowed ground."

Desiree swore in Italian and she made an odd gesture with her hand, something to ward off evil. It occurred to me that she could swear in three different languages and I found that vaguely impressive.

"And," I went on, "the family would have had to be rich to pay the monks to look the other way. You know, so that they could bury their loved one as close as possible to hallowed ground. It's about the right time period. And the Capulets were a rich family."

"Seriously?"

"Seriously."

"So you think it really could have been Juliet? In there?"

"I don't know. It could be."

Desiree stared at me for a long moment. She put a hand on the stone. "It's warm," she said. "The stones are warm."

I touched them. "Weird," I said.

"I can imagine how she must have felt," said Desiree.

"Huh?"

"She was trapped. She would rather die than live a life she didn't choose."

"I don't know that it—"

"I'm the same way. You need to know that." Desiree held me in her gaze. "I have to live my life in my own way, not according to anyone else's rules."

"Okay," I said.

She let her camera hang from the strap around her neck. "Can we get out of here now?"

"Okay," I said.

She was solemn as we trundled up the stairs. At the top, the sun slanted down through the old cloisters. The clouds had lifted and a bird was singing in the high branches of the oak tree. We strode back out to the street and Verona clattered to life all around us.

———

The office was bustling when we arrived. A number of women looked up from the round table when I walked in with Desiree. I didn't recognize any of them. Giovanna was behind the counter, and on the near side, a thin woman held a sheaf of papers and was addressing the group. Her papers rattled and her eyes darted. Through the crowd, Anna drifted into view. She waved when she saw us and we shuffled over to where she was standing. The thin woman grimaced at the interruption.

"Buon giorno," Anna whispered. "Is this Desiree?"

"Yes," I said.

"Hi," said Desiree.

The woman by the counter glared at us but continued to read from her papers.

"Let's go to the back," said Anna. "We can talk there."

"What's going on?" I whispered. We followed Anna down the hallway, and at the door to her office she stopped. She glanced quickly at me and then sized up Desiree.

"It's the first meeting," Anna said.

"The first meeting of what?"

Her eyes turned back on me. "Probably I have told you about Juliet's birthday. We are beginning the planning."

"And who was that woman speaking?" I asked.

"That is Barbara," Anna said. "She will be organizing the celebration this year."

Desiree murmured something in Italian and Anna looked a bit surprised, then burst into a conspiratorial chuckle. They exchanged a few more whispered words, glancing at me and then laughing.

"Hey," I said. "No fair."

Out front, Barbara plowed on until something in her speech caught Anna's attention.

"I'm sorry," Anna said. "She is passing out the papers now. I think I must go back."

"Okay," I said. "We'll just get to work on the letters."

"No, you must come too," said Anna.

She turned me around and gave me a little push down the hall to the front. People were chattering now. The papers rustled and flapped as they were passed around. Anna took one and passed the very last one to me. It was a schedule of sorts, marked with times and languages. At the top it read *"Compleanno di Giulietta."*

"What is this?" I asked Anna.

"For the birthday celebration, we always read from the letters—in many different languages."

Barbara called for quiet again and I felt Desiree tuck in beside me. Barbara rattled through the schedule, then her gaze turned on me. She spoke directly at me, in Italian.

"Glenn," Giovanna said, translating, "you will read the English letter at Juliet's birthday."

"Me?"

"Yes. We would like this," she said.

Barbara waited patiently.

"But, I'm not . . ." I began, but Desiree nudged me.

Everyone in the room was staring at me. Then Desiree squeezed my arm. I could tell she was excited for me and wanted me to say yes.

"What do I have to do?" I asked.

"You will read the English letter," said Giovanna, "in the Piazza dei Signori."

"In the piazza? But how many people are going to be there?"

"All of Verona," said Giovanna. "All of Verona will be there."

"Oh, I don't know . . ."

"Glenn," whispered Desiree, "you should be honored that they're asking you."

"All right," I said, but everyone's attention had already turned back to Barbara.

When the meeting finally broke apart, Desiree and I shuffled back to our office down the hall.

"They must like you," said Desiree.

"I don't know about that."

"Of course they do. They're impressed by you."

"Who said that?"

"No one. They don't have to. It's obvious."

On the desk, the cardboard box was overflowing again. Someone must have refilled it. We rearranged the chairs, side by side, so that when we sat our knees touched under the desktop.

A few minutes later, Anna appeared at the door. "Everyone is leaving for lunch," she announced. She was pulling on her coat. "But I am going home for the day."

"Everything okay?"

"Yes, of course," she said, though something looked amiss. "I will see you tomorrow?" she asked.

"Sure."

"I will go to the new office tomorrow afternoon. Probably, I will collect the letters from the letter box first. Would you like to meet me there?"

"At Juliet's house?" Desiree asked.

"Yes. You will come?"

"Of course," said Desiree.

"And Glenn," said Anna, "I will have a surprise for you there."

"A surprise?" I said.

Anna waved her hand. "Tomorrow. We can say three o'clock? At the letter box."

———

Desiree and I chipped away at the letters. It grew quiet out front, and I think maybe we were the only ones left in the office. Half an hour later, I came to an astonishing letter. "Dear Juliet," it began. "My name is Fiona. I'm twenty-three and currently traveling in Europe. We've had a day trip to Verona, and so I wrote you this note. I was born with a lung disease called cystic fibrosis and my health is now declining quickly. There is no cure for this disease."

"Oh," I said, out loud.

Desiree looked up from her own letter. She watched my face fall. "Are you okay?" she asked.

"I just . . . well, I've never seen one like this before." I tapped at the letter in front of me and read some more.

"I am in love with a man named Danny. He's twenty-five and we want to get married. If you believe in soul mates, he is mine. I don't know if our parents will allow us to marry and I wonder if it is fair to him. Already it is very hard for me to breathe. I probably won't live to be forty, and my last years will not be good. Is it okay for me to just accept that I will have a tragic love story in the end? He says yes but I don't know."

"What is it?" Desiree asked.

The last two lines of the letter read: "All my love is on these two sheets of paper. Treat them well."

"Oh shit," I said. I could feel my throat constricting.

"What does it say?" she asked, reaching for the letter. She scanned it and her eyes grew liquid. Then she stood up abruptly. "I have to go outside," she mumbled. She toppled out of the office and disappeared. I sat for a moment then went after her. Out front, her face had drained of color. She was not quite crying but it was close.

190

She stared at her feet, not saying anything. Then she looked up at me with a lost expression on her face.

"What is it?" I asked.

"I almost died," she said.

"What?"

"I was fifteen." She gulped in a breath of air. "They rushed me to the hospital in an ambulance."

"Jesus. What happened?"

"I had a severe allergic reaction. I couldn't breathe." She shook her head. "My skin turned bright red like a boiled lobster. Except for my fingernails—they were blue. Then . . . then . . ."

"It's okay," I said. I reached for her, palming my hand on her shoulder.

"I'd had allergic reactions before, but they were getting progressively worse each time. This one almost killed me, so I thought the next one . . ."

"What caused it?"

"Walnuts," she said. "Stupid walnuts. I'm allergic to all nuts, but some are worse than others. Some will kill me." She gulped in another breath and calmed a little. "After that, I decided to live my life the way I wanted. If it was going to be short, then I didn't want to die with any regrets."

"That's not such a bad way to live."

"And here I am," she said. "I'm still alive, a full-grown adult. And I'm lost. I'm lost, Glenn. I don't know what I'm doing. I've lived all over the world but I don't feel like I belong anywhere."

She looked totally despondent in that moment. There was nothing I could say to help. "Come here." I wrapped my arms around her and she sank into me.

"You are still here," I whispered into her ear. "And you're in Italy again."

She pulled away from me a little. "This was where I came first," she said. "Italy. I wanted to live here, and you know how that worked out." She shook her head. "Nothing in my life has turned out the way I expected."

"Maybe nobody's life turns out how they expect it."

"I know, but . . ."

"Are you going to be all right?"

"Yeah." She wiped at the corner of her eye.

"Giovanna will probably be back soon," I said. "Should we . . . ?"

She nodded and trailed after me, back to our office.

The letter from Fiona was still sitting on the desk, slightly askew. I thumped down into my chair. "Maybe," I said, "we'll just answer this one later."

Desiree sat, expressionless.

"Here," I said, pulling in a sheet of the Club di Giulietta stationery toward me. I hunched over it, writing a sentence in the bottom corner by the graphic of Juliet. Desiree watched me. I reached for a pair of scissors and cut off the strip I'd written on. On the paper, in my very best printing, I had written, "*To thine own self be true.*" I passed the tiny scroll to Desiree.

"What's that for?" she asked.

"For your locket," I said.

Her fingers were already on the locket, opening the latch.

It fit perfectly.

———

That night, Desiree and I bought tickets to the opera. I didn't tell her that I'd gone the year before and that it had been a colossal letdown. Then again, this time we were seeing *Aida*, not *Romeo and Juliet*.

The performance didn't start until dark, so we strolled around the piazza in the gathering dusk, the sky above us a delicate, pale blue. A single star floated above rooftops and in the distance the coliseum heaved itself up, ancient and foreboding.

192

I realize I haven't done this remarkable place justice. The coliseum, first of all, is literally at the center of Verona in a vast cobblestone square called the Piazza Brà. At one end of the piazza sits the neoclassical city hall. At the other end, the place is lined with cafés, like Paris, with outdoor tables where you can sit and watch people promenade by.

In the middle, though, the Roman coliseum rears up above everything else. This stadium once held thirty thousand people. The pink-and-white limestone blocks were quarried from the nearby hills of Valpolicella and they reflect the sky, leaden in the rain but a shimmering ethereal light in the sunshine. About a thousand years ago, the outer curtain wall collapsed in an earthquake, so what's left is a central structure of two levels. Each level features seventy-two arches, and each arch is as big as a train tunnel. Around the back, near the ticket office, the only remaining wall from the original outer ring still stands, rising up another level above the rest, and there you can fully appreciate the glory that was Rome.

Desiree was entranced. We'd dressed up for the opera, and when she'd first come out of her room at Emiliano's, wearing a yellow summer dress, her hair shimmering and cascading down her shoulders, I had fumbled for words. "Wow" was all I could manage.

"You just smarten it up, mister," she said, but her eyes were dancing.

We melted into the tuxedoed crowds milling about the entrance. I'd forgotten to bring something for us to sit on, so I steered Desiree toward a stall that sold cushions and we bought a couple. I also picked up a little maroon booklet that described the story of *Aida*—with the complete libretto in both the original Italian and in English on the facing page. We strode in through one of the train-tunnel archways, up a set of weathered marble stairs to our seats near the top of the stadium. I couldn't help but think of all those who had climbed these steps before us—those who had come to see the gladiators and staged hunts of exotic animals.

Tonight, it was the story of an Egyptian slave girl who fell in love with a captain in the army. The music is some of the greatest ever composed, the masterpiece of Giuseppe Verdi, and the crowd was buzzing with excitement. We sat high up to the left of the stage with some fifteen thousand people filling the seats below us. To the west, the sun had already set in an apricot sky and, as it bruised and darkened, a dozen klieg spotlights blasted up into the night, bright shafts of illumination that flickered back and forth across the clouds. Hawkers sold cold beer and water and popcorn. Across from us, the outer ring of Roman arches rose above the crowds, the old stones silhouetted in purple. And as the warm night settled over us and the crowds stilled, the people below us began to light tiny handheld candles. The klieg lights shuttered off and in the blackness, the candles glimmered, tens of thousands of them, like stars. Desiree leaned into me.

A single spotlight illuminated the conductor, who marched onto the stage, tails flapping, a sweep of long gray hair bouncing off his shoulders. The crowd roared as he stepped onto a podium. He raised his baton, and the glorious music began.

The stage lights came up and we were in a palace complex in ancient Egypt. Painted columns lined a throne room, and in the middle of it all sat the great pharaoh. The string section swelled and a long line of ghostly figures paraded out onto the stage. Behind them the palace complex rose, four or five stories tall, with figures scurrying up into it, Egyptian soldiers, all a part of the story, clutching spears that flashed in the stage lights.

Of course the singing was in Italian, and even Desiree soon pressed over to read along in my maroon booklet. At one point, about a hundred slave girls in diaphanous gowns performed a ballet. They swept around the pharaoh like gusts of wind. Desiree had been a ballerina herself. She watched, enthralled, shuffling over closer to me as the evening cooled, until her shoulder was nestled into mine.

It was almost eleven o'clock by the time the first intermission was called, and when the lights blinked on, the crowd bustled around us, standing, laughing, heading for the exits. "Fifteen minutes," Desiree said, translating the announcement that had come over the sound system.

"Let's go stretch our legs," I said. It felt good to get up, to join the streams funneling down the timeworn steps. It didn't take long until we were out on the piazza again. We walked past the props for the other operas, and arrived at an archway that was lit up. It must have been a dressing room, because a dozen or so men lounged there, all wearing Egyptian headdresses, their eyes lined with dark kohl, smoking cigarettes and chatting. One sat on a wooden kitchen chair outside the archway checking texts on his iPhone. He looked up as we passed, this character from three thousand years ago, the blue glow of his phone shimmering on his painted face.

The crowds spilled around us, revelers in jeans and silver-haired men in tuxedos, their hair-sprayed wives on their arms, all pearls and evening dresses. We weaved through them, farther out into the darkness, across the cobblestones, to a low fountain, and we sat on its ledge.

I opened the little maroon booklet.

"What happens next?" asked Desiree.

"Wouldn't you like to know?" I held the booklet up and away from her.

"Hey!" she said, laughing, snatching the book out of my hands. She read some lines out loud. *"Farewell, thou vale of sorrow. Brief dream of joy condemned to end in woe."*

She heaved an exaggerated sigh. "Why do all these love stories have such sad endings?"

"Stories need drama," I said.

"I don't need any more drama."

"No, me neither." It occurred to me then that I had let go of some of my sorrow. I wasn't thinking about Claire anymore. I was here, now, in the present. And at that moment, I really didn't want to be anywhere else.

A gong sounded. "Time to go back," Desiree said.

The second scene of act 2 began with the triumphal entry of soldiers, hundreds of them, a row of desolate prisoners between the columns, spear points edged into their haggard backs. A march boomed out from the orchestra pit, a martial blast of victory. And then came the horses, great white stallions, heads held high, prancing, golden harnesses sparkling in the glare of the stage lights.

If I had to guess, I'd say there were three hundred performers on the stage.

"Spectacular," I said. Below us, Aida made her plans to escape into the desert, to flee with the one she loved. In the next scene, a boat drifted along the Nile and an aria arose. The audience began to sing along, a chorus of several thousand people rumbling behind the orchestra like thunder. I felt a shuddering chill zipper down the back of my neck at the beauty of it all.

By the time it ended, Aida and her lover were imprisoned in a vault, doomed to their deaths, almost like Romeo and Juliet, and a quiet grief fell over the crowd. And as the opera drew to a close, even as the last strains of the violins lapped across the ancient stones, the stage lights dimmed and the entire coliseum stood deathly silent for a moment, until a roar erupted, a bellow of approval and shouts of Bravo! Bravo! Bravo! The applause went on for ten long minutes, the conductor forced to walk the length of the stage twice, probably fifty yards from the wings to the podium, while the crowd chanted and clapped. Desiree had her hand up over her mouth, mesmerized. "Amazing," she said. "Absolutely amazing."

It was well after midnight when we spilled back onto the piazza. Taxis shunted the curb, though most of the concertgoers seemed to just drift off into the night.

Sometimes, I thought, the real magic is not in the spectacular.

Sometimes it's much more subtle. After the crowds and the timpani and the oratorios, we walked through the gates of the medieval walls, the stars above us, and Desiree's hand slipped quietly into mine.

———

The next morning, a sunbeam slanted in through my window. I came to with a start and realized it was already late. I dressed quickly and stumbled out to the front room. Desiree was sitting at our breakfast table, long finished eating, working on her laptop.

"Good morning, sunshine," she said.

I wanted to say something, but all that came out was a grunt.

"We have a free day," she said. "Giovanna e-mailed to say not to bother coming in this morning."

"Really?"

"But we're still meeting Anna at three," she said.

"So what do you want to do?'

"See more of Verona, don't you think?"

"Sure."

She stood up. "How about I show you the Italy I know."

"Okay." I wasn't sure what she meant.

"First," she said, "we go to a bar."

"A bar? Isn't it kind of early?"

"A coffee bar for cappuccino and *bomboloni*."

"What's that?"

"Pastries," she said, "with cream inside. You just wait."

We headed west, into a part of Verona I didn't know. Desiree was in a buoyant mood. She skipped along at a good clip, her face alight. "It's great to be here," she said. "I really didn't think I would ever come back."

"Because of Rafael?"

"Yeah, mostly. He was a huge part of my life here. We thought we were soul mates. It was us against the world." She gave a sort of half chuckle. "Did you know in Italy it's bad luck to get married on a Tuesday?"

"So you got married on a Tuesday."

"Yeah. We didn't care."

"Why did you get married at all?"

"There," she said. "There's a coffee bar." She beelined across the street and we went into a little shop. It smelled of old wood and coffee beans. A few men were leaning against the bar, one reading a newspaper, two others engaged in conversation. Desiree said something to the man behind the bar and he swung off to the espresso machine, an ancient thing with levers and dials, and steam hissing out of a pipe. She pressed in against the bar, just like the men. "I needed the marriage certificate," she said, picking up the conversation again. "So I could keep my visa, you know. That was the only reason we got married."

Our coffees arrived in mugs no bigger than teacups. And then came two small plates, each with a paper doily under a fat, round pastry. They were coated in icing sugar and still warm from the oven.

She stared at her cappuccino but didn't reach for it yet. "Within the first year, everything changed. Everybody thought of us as a married couple—except for the two of us. The worst thing was being called Rafael's wife. I hated that."

I poured some sugar into my coffee and waited for her to continue.

"It's just . . . it was family, I guess. In Italy everything is about the family. You have to know that. His family had a business and he . . . Well, his family wouldn't let him go. I finally realized that he would never leave his little town. He couldn't."

"I'm sorry," I said.

"Almost ten years have passed," she said. "A long time. I did a master's degree. I went back to my original plan of working toward a PhD but . . . I don't know, that didn't completely work out either."

I took a sip of my coffee. It was so powerful I winced.

"There's more," she said. "There's something else I should probably tell you."

Now what?

She had just begun to speak when the cathedral bells started ringing, a long string of them. When they finally tapered off into silence, I said, "You were going to tell me something."

"Ah, no," she said. "Don't worry about it." She reached for her cappuccino. "Let's just enjoy the rest of the day."

———

After that, we wandered the cobblestone streets. I steered her away from the Casa di Giulietta knowing that we'd be there at three to meet Anna. By two o'clock, the sun was high in a bright blue sky. It was still a little cool for early September, but at least the rain had stopped.

We picked up some pizza to go from another little shop. The slices were square and wrapped in thick brown paper so they wouldn't drip on you. One street over, we found a tiny square with a covered portico where we could sit and eat our pizza. Washing hung from a line on a window above us and, across from the pillars, a green door had a knocker of brass in the shape of a small human head. Behind us, a knot of children took turns kicking a soccer ball against a wall.

"I still think a lot about my students," I said, watching the kids. "I remember this one assignment I used to give before *Romeo and Juliet*. It was a sort of questionnaire you had to answer. It wasn't for marks."

"A questionnaire about what?" Desiree peeled back the paper and took a bite of her pizza.

"It was about your internal locus of control."

"About your what?"

"Internal locus of control. It means how much control you think you have over your own life versus the outside things controlling you. Fate, I guess."

Desiree considered her pizza.

"All the students had to answer this questionnaire, then add up their responses to get a number on a scale. I can't remember, but I think it was something like one to thirty."

She took another small bite.

"The lower the number, the more you believe you have complete control over your life, the higher the number, the more you believe that external forces control your life."

"Did you do it yourself?" asked Desiree. It was a good question.

"Yes," I said.

"And?"

"I scored a nine."

"So you don't believe in fate."

"No, not really."

"But a nine," she said, "doesn't that mean you believe just a little?"

"Here's the thing. This test, the instructions on it, said that a seven or an eight is just about optimal. It's the healthiest, mentally speaking."

Desiree scrunched up her nose. "Why?"

"Apparently most of the CEOs of major corporations are sevens or eights. Billionaires are almost always sevens."

"Not sure that makes them better people."

"No."

"Are you going to eat your pizza?" she asked.

I looked at my slice. The cheese was cooling, but it still smelled quite good. "I guess," I went on, trying to finish my thoughts, "just the belief that you can control things allows you to be more successful."

"Maybe," she said. "But some things are definitely out of our control. I don't care what anyone says."

The kids had stopped kicking the soccer ball. One small boy was looking over at us. I took a bite of my pizza.

"Like this," Desiree said.

"Like what?"

"Like us." She held my gaze. "C'mon now," she said. "Don't make me spell it out for you."

I searched her face, looking for more, but she was inscrutable.

"I think if I did that quiz," she went on, "I'd probably score about fifteen—because I don't really believe we have as much control as you think we do."

"Maybe," I said.

"Like Claire, for example," she said.

I clenched a little. It still hurt to hear that name. "What about her?"

"Once Claire found out she was pregnant, she didn't have a lot of options."

"I've thought about that. I suppose it was like dominoes. She had to do what she had to do."

"You're a guy. You have no idea. It was a lot harder for her than it was for you."

"Yeah, I know. I get that." I put the envelope of pizza down on the ledge beside me. Suddenly, I didn't feel hungry anymore. "All I'm saying," I said, "is that you have to believe you have some control over your own life. You have to believe that even if fate takes something from you, it's up to you to get beyond it. It's up to you to find the happy ending."

Desiree had finished her own slice. She crunched the paper into a ball and looked around for a garbage can. I watched her for a moment.

"What?" she said.

"Nothing." Actually, I wanted to ask her about before—when she said there was something more she needed to tell me.

"It must be almost three," she said. "We should probably get going."

Desiree and I crossed the Piazza delle Erbe, past the Roman statue and the fruit stands, and walked down the Via Cappello to Juliet's house. I knew the shortcut into the courtyard but I wanted Desiree to enter under the archway. The passageway, maybe five meters long, is almost a tunnel. It's thronged with tourists, but it still feels magical to emerge from the darkness and find yourself in the ancient courtyard.

When we arrived, Desiree angled her camera up at the famous balcony and clicked off a burst. I'd told her it wasn't real but it didn't matter. It was beautiful. In fact, it came to me just then that if Romeo were looking up at this balcony, he would indeed be facing east. *It is the east*, he says, *and Juliet is the sun*.

"Look up there, above the passageway where we entered. Do you see it?" I said.

Desiree raised her camera and zoomed in on the coat of arms above the entrance. The carving was worn with the years and no bigger than a dinner plate, but it was the ancient insignia of the Cappello family. "That, at least, is real," I said. "That's how they know that this was the house of the Cappello family."

"Looks a bit like a bowler hat," she said.

"It is a hat, or a cap, I guess, and it's been up there for seven hundred years." I checked my watch. "We have some time. Do you want to go inside?"

"Is it less crowded in there?" The courtyard was swarming with people.

"It's usually pretty empty."

"Then let's go."

Things were much the same as last year. An older woman took our euros and I showed Desiree the original statue of Juliet up on the landing, the right breast cracked like a broken vase. We clomped up the wooden stairs and at the top came into the large room where, supposedly, Romeo and Juliet first met.

"I never really did get a chance to tell my students about all this," I said.

"Why not?"

"I don't know. It seemed like there was such a difference between what was real and what was just a story."

"What's that supposed to mean?"

I followed her across the plank floor to where a massive fireplace stood. Two high-backed chairs stood in front of it. "Well," I said, "it's like Juliet's statue—actually I didn't realize until after—it's one of the main points of the story. Everyone forgets about that."

"The statue?'

"Lord Montague—Romeo's father—says he will put up a statue of Juliet, to honor her, and I suppose to show that the fighting between the two families is over. That's the happy ending."

Desiree adjusted something on her camera. She walked to the corner of the room to get it all into the shot. I trailed behind her. "It's not that happy an ending," she said.

"No," I said. "I guess not." I sighed quite audibly.

She peered at me over her viewfinder.

"What?"

"I was thinking . . ."

"Yes?"

"Maybe it's what Shakespeare was trying to say all along. Maybe you have to go through some sort of hell before you can come out on the other side. Before you can change your thinking and yourself."

She tucked her head down again and snapped off a shot.

"What I mean," I said, "is that it's the same for me. It took a disaster for me to finally let go of a love that was never going to happen, to finally come out on the other side."

She straightened and faced me.

"And then," I said, "you came along."

"That's right, Mr. Destiny." In the soft light, she grinned and bent again to check the settings on her camera.

"You know," I said, "the balcony is right over there."

A Venetian archway just off the main room led into a little side room. And there a door opened onto the famous balcony. "Shall we?" I asked.

"Go out on it?"

"Yes."

We emerged into the sunshine, Desiree blinking in the light. From the balcony we could see out over the rooftops. Beside us, a sweep of ivy crept up the wall and over us.

Someone called out below. Then a chorus of voices echoed.

"What are they saying?" I asked.

"They want us to kiss," she said.

I leaned forward and gave her the slightest kiss on the lips.

"Can we go now?" she said.

"Okay."

Just inside, she stopped. She looked angry. "That's not the real one," she insisted.

"The real what?" I asked.

"I'm not kissing you just because I've been told to."

I laughed.

"Don't make fun."

"I'm not. I think it's kind of sweet."

"Just remember: That one didn't count. That's not the real one."

We descended the wooden steps and emerged into the courtyard. The crowds had shifted enough that nobody recognized us as the couple up on the balcony a few minutes before. I heard my name being called, then saw Anna standing by the letter box, waving at us. Had she seen us on the balcony? I didn't think so. Beside her stood Soňa, grinning and waving. It took a moment to register. "Soňa!" I cried.

"Who?" said Desiree.

"It's Soňa. Soňa has come back."

I pushed through the crowds, dragging Desiree along with me. We edged around one last group and arrived at the letter box. "Soňa," I said, "what are you doing here?" She looked the same. High cheekbones, blond hair dyed copper at the tips, a jangle of bracelets on either wrist.

"I have come," said Soňa, "for Juliet's birthday."

"Desiree," I said, tugging her in close beside me. "This is Soňa. She was here last year writing letters with me."

"Hi," said Desiree.

"Soňa has agreed to read a letter at the ceremony," said Anna. "If we can find a Czech one."

"Of course we can find a Czech letter," said Soňa. "There are sixteen million of us."

"Probably we should open the box now," Anna declared. She dangled the key over the padlock and Soňa snatched it from her. The same old Laurel and Hardy show.

"Wait," said Desiree. "Let me take a photo."

Soňa waited a moment, then clinked off the padlock and swung the letter box open. Anna shoveled out the letters into a canvas bag. We escaped through a door to the right of the letter box. The owners of that shop were the keepers of the key, and Soňa dropped it off. Then we were through and back on the street again. Anna walked ahead, swinging the bag of letters as she walked. Desiree and Soňa stepped along with me.

We crossed the Piazza delle Erbe again, and it was all so much like last year. On the other side of the square, up between two ancient buildings, I could see the whale bone hanging like a sword over the pedestrians.

"How are your studies going?" I asked Soňa.

"They are going," she said. "I am still working on my master's degree."

"What are you studying?" asked Desiree.

"Italian language and literature," said Soňa.

They sprang into step together, ahead of me, chatting away like two old friends.

When we got to the new office, we poured the letters out onto the wooden table and began to sort through them. We worked quietly, pulling letters out from the piles, one by one, pens scribbling, heads down.

"Listen to this one," Soňa said, breaking the silence. "Dear Juliet, I am sure my boyfriend is seeing other girls. My friend Angela says she saw him at a movie with another girl."

"Save yourself some sorrow, sister," Desiree said.

"Yeah, dump him," Soňa agreed. "Immediately."

"But you can't write that," I said.

"Okay, okay," said Soňa. "How about 'Dear Linda, you must be careful in love. You must find out the truth, but most of all, you must guard your own heart.'"

"That's good," I said.

"Yes," said Desiree. "Very diplomatic."

"How do you come up with this stuff?" I asked.

Soňa became serious. "I think a lot about it. I think you need to know yourself first before you can fall in real love—and before someone can fall in love with you. It's like once you are in love with yourself, then others can follow your example."

"That's actually quite brilliant," I said.

Desiree drew a hand up to her locket. "*To thine own self be true*," she said.

"*And*," I continued, "*it must follow, as the night the day, thou canst not then be false to any man.*"

I fumbled for a moment, reaching inside my backpack. "Maybe now is a good time," I said, "for a more difficult letter. We read this one yesterday." I placed the letter from Fiona, the girl with cystic fibrosis, on the table.

Desiree turned pale.

"We don't know how to answer it."

"Read it," said Soňa.

I read the whole thing aloud and ended with those powerful two lines: "All my love is on these two sheets of paper. Treat them well."

I pulled out a blank sheet of stationery and squared it in front of me.

"First of all, you must say that we all read her letter," said Soňa.

"Okay," I said and began to write.

"Probably," said Anna, "you can write that this is the saddest letter we have ever read."

"Maybe not saddest, maybe another word?" said Desiree.

"Most beautiful?" I glanced up at her.

"Most poignant," Desiree said, and with that word, the rest of the letter came to us line by line. In the end, we had this:

Dear Fiona,

We have read your letter. I hope you don't mind, but we shared it amongst ourselves, all the secretaries of Juliet. It is the most poignant letter any of us has yet read. And for some time, we didn't know how to answer. What we can say is this: You remind us how fragile and precious our time is here on this earth. So treasure every moment. Sing with your deepest heart, every note. Cherish your time with Danny; he sounds like a good man. Our hearts go out to you, and may you have many years of happiness.

"How should I sign it?" I asked.

"You should sign, 'The secretaries of Juliet,'" Soňa advised.

"Yes," I said. I penned the words in the best handwriting I could manage. "This one is from all of us."

9

Of all days in the year

A couple of days before Juliet's birthday, we were called in for a final meeting at the old office. I was hoping we'd be dressed up in medieval costumes to look like the characters in the Zeffirelli film. Instead, when Desiree and I arrived, Barbara stood guard at the front door with a clipboard and a pained expression. She passed a letter to me, the letter I'd have to read out loud in the square. My name was penciled in at the top, spelled wrong.

Barbara lifted up a second letter, handing this one to Desiree. Desiree stared at the paper for a moment and was about to protest when someone else crowded in behind us and we were pushed forward into the foyer. The place was swarming with people and the chatter was boisterous, like a cocktail party in full swing.

"Well," said Desiree, flapping the paper, "looks like I have to read a letter too."

"It just means they like you."

"Very funny." She shook her head. "I don't know. I'm terrified of speaking in public."

I started reading my own letter. The first sentence was littered with mistakes. "Damn," I said. "Look at this."

"It's been translated," Desiree said, leaning in to me to read it. "Badly. I can probably fix that for you."

"What did you get?" I asked.

Desiree scanned her letter. "The usual. A young woman pining for love." She looked around the room. "Who are all these people?"

"I have no idea."

There were a few other men in the room, something I'd not seen before, and with them stood Giulio Tamassia. "Hey." I nudged Desiree. "Over there. That's Giovanna's father. He started the Club di Giulietta." Giulio stood imperiously, presiding over a conversation, a bright red tie draping down his chest. Almost as if he'd heard me, Giulio's gaze traveled across to us. Manuela stood beside him. He whispered something to her, then broke from his group and edged around the table, moving toward us, his eyes locked on Desiree.

"*Boun giorno,*" Desiree said as he rounded on us.

"*Buon giorno,*" I echoed. Giulio all but ignored me.

"*Sono Desiree,*" Desiree said, extending her hand.

"*Piacere,*" said Giulio. He shook her hand flamboyantly. I stepped away, bumping into the photocopier machine behind me. Giulio rested his hand on her forearm and said something that made her laugh. He looked over at me once, frowning, and he leaned in closer and said something quietly. She chuckled again.

Barbara swept into the room then, clapping and calling for everyone to quiet down. Giulio excused himself and went back to where he'd been standing before.

"What was that all about?" I whispered.

"He said he was glad that I was here."

"And . . . ?"

"He asked where I was from. If I'm from an Italian family."

"That's it?"

She paused. "He asked about you too."

"What did he say?"

"He asked if you were really a teacher of Shakespeare."

"And what did you say?"

"That, yes, you'd been a teacher for almost twenty years. I think he was impressed."

"He didn't look like it."

Barbara clapped again and the room settled. She read out the names of the letter readers from her clipboard, and, one by one, people stood to be acknowledged. She read my name and then Desiree's, and we raised our hands gamely. There were many more people in the room than just those reading letters though. I'd never seen the office so crowded.

Anna appeared behind us. *"Buon giorno,"* she said. "You have your letters?"

"Yes, thanks."

Standing near Giulio was another man, a stout man, dressed as if he'd just arrived from Oktoberfest. He stroked his manicured beard and plucked at his suspenders theatrically. He was clearly trying to catch my eye.

"Anna, who's that guy? He keeps staring at me."

"He will be your actor," said Anna.

"My what?"

"And Desiree, your actor will be Edvige." Anna gestured to an impeccably dressed woman with a silk scarf around her neck. She smiled at us.

"But what do you mean, actors?" I asked

"Ah," she said. "You will read the letter in your language, then your actor will read the translation in Italian."

211

"Do we get to wear costumes?"

"Costumes?" said Anna. "No, that is not on the plan."

Barbara was about to start again. She raised her clipboard, but before she could speak, Giulio slipped in behind her and said something into her ear. She stopped and Guilio stepped forward. The room hushed immediately. He spoke a few words directly to me, pinning me with his eyes. Of course, it was all in Italian, so I didn't understand anything. When he finished, everyone in the room was staring at me. It had gone completely silent.

Giovanna spoke up. "Glenn," she said, "my father says you should read from Shakespeare—in the piazza." It wasn't a question.

"Me?"

"Yes. He thinks it is a good idea."

Giulio waited. He looked like a grandfather who had just given some important advice, and was watching now to make sure it had sunk in.

"Okay, I guess."

Giulio tipped his head as if to say, *See, wasn't that easy?* and before I could say anything more, Barbara broke in, moving on to the next topic. Desiree laid her hand on my arm. She squeezed it once. "Shakespeare," she whispered. "You will be reading from Shakespeare."

Barbara described the rest of the program. Manuela's daughter would perform a ballet. There'd be artists and musicians, and the birthday celebration would go on all afternoon.

When the meeting finally ended, everyone streamed out into the parking lot, some to smoke cigarettes, some to chat, others to escape in their cars or on their bicycles. Manuela bustled toward me with another of the men I'd seen in the room. I'd seen him standing by the front door, a bald man with a little notebook in his hand. He'd stood apart from the others as Barbara issued her orders.

"Glenn," said Manuela, "may I present Mr. Jenkins."

"Hello," I said.

"Jolyon Jenkins," he said, "with the BBC." He stepped forward to shake my hand. He wore a beige vest with pockets running up the front, the kind you see fishermen wearing, or maybe war correspondents on assignment.

"I'm with Radio Four," he said. "We'll be recording a program for Juliet's birthday."

"Really?" I thought of the Korean Broadcasting Service, so long ago. Manuela said, "I will be taking Mr. Jenkins on the tour of the city this afternoon."

He nodded graciously. "And I am very much looking forward to it."

"But," said Manuela, "I thought you should first meet each other. Glenn," she said, "is an expert on *Romeo and Juliet*."

"Well, I'm not really an expert."

"Then, I should like to interview you at some point," he said.

"For the BBC?"

"If that is quite all right with you."

"Yes, yes, I'm sorry. Of course. It's just a lot to take in."

"We must be going. We have many things to see," she said. "And you? What is your program for the day?"

"I'm not sure," I said. "Any suggestions?"

"You have seen San Zeno?"

"What's San Zeno?"

Manuela smiled. "It is the cathedral, on the other side of the river. Some say Romeo and Juliet were married there in the crypt. Perhaps you should visit it."

———

The Basilica di San Zeno Maggiore is as old a cathedral as you are likely to find in Europe. The crypt holds the mummified remains of Saint Zeno, the patron saint of Verona who lived here almost seventeen centuries ago. The cathedral itself is more than a thousand years old, constructed of cream-colored stones. A massive stained-glass window called the Wheel of Fortune is set in the bricks above the front doors.

A wedding ceremony had just concluded when Desiree and I arrived, and the guests were pouring out onto the steps. It could have been a wedding anywhere—uncles in stiff suits, bridesmaids in taffeta, kids skipping and oblivious to the occasion. The bride and groom emerged into a hail of confetti and the popping of flashbulbs. Did they realize they were being married in what might have been the same place as Romeo and Juliet? Did they know how that story ended? Desiree and I had been holding hands on the way to the cathedral, but she dropped my hand like a rock when she saw the bride and groom. It wasn't even a Tuesday.

The two of us skirted the crowds and entered the cathedral through a side entrance. Inside, bouquets of white roses and delicate purple gladiolas were being packed into boxes. An old man swept up the petals and debris, growling to himself at the mess. He disappeared down a stairwell with his broom and dustpan and an eerie silence hung over the great empty cathedral.

"Do you want your camera?" I asked Desiree. I carried it in my daypack. The damn thing was heavy.

"Maybe later," she said.

We headed up the side of the nave, with the long wooden pews to the right of us. Stout marble pillars striped horizontally in chalk-white and puce rose almost up to the ceiling, and there, between the old timber braces, were the stars. Six-sided stars, exactly the same as the ones at Juliet's house, hundreds of them lining the roof in alternating colors of mustard yellow and silver. The stars were older than Shakespeare, older even than Dante.

"That's where the idea comes from," I said, craning my neck up at them. "The whole star-crossed-lovers thing."

Desiree was circumspect, oddly silent. After a while, she said, "Do you really think they were married here?"

"Supposedly the wedding took place in the crypt. You know, to keep it hidden."

We shuffled up the aisle, our footsteps echoing, toward the front of the cathedral and the apse. Over the stone altarpiece hung a renaissance masterpiece by Andrea Mantegna, a triptych of images with Mary on a throne in the center panel holding up the Christ child. The ancient paint had taken on a black sheen that was almost lustrous. To the side of the apse, in a round niche, a statue of Saint Zeno grinned down at us. A set of steps beside him led down to a subterranean room. "That's got to be it," I said.

The color had drained from Desiree's face.

"Look," I said, "I'll just pop down for a moment. You can stay up here."

"No," she said, "I'm going if you're going."

I edged down the stairs and Desiree clamped on to my arm, a step behind me. The crypt was actually well lit. Most of the room was taken up with a sort of golden cage, and behind the latticework, the saint's wooden sarcophagus sat in a spotlight. It looked like a gilded aquarium.

A full-size cast of the saint reclined behind a window in the sarcophagus. It looked like a mannequin coated in silver and dressed in red velvet robes. A bishop's miter sat like a crown on the sterling head, except that the point of it stuck out horizontally, like a folded linen napkin that had fallen from the table. I assume the cast encased his bones. I'd read that on the feast day of San Zeno, the townspeople hauled the cast up and paraded it through the city. I hadn't told Desiree that. She was spooked enough as it was.

"So that's him?" she asked.

"Yeah," I said. "That's him."

She pressed in closer. I could feel her breath on my neck.

"This is so creepy," she said.

The place was nothing like the movie scenes. I remembered

teaching the wedding scene, the danger that was inherent in it for everybody: Romeo and Juliet kiss, of course, but Friar Lawrence stands
back from it all. *These violent delights,* he says, *have violent ends. And in
their triumph die, like fire.*

Desiree sighed. "I don't ever want to get married again," she said.

"Well, not here for sure."

"Not anywhere."

"Okay, well, that's exercising your internal locus of control."

"Are you making fun of me?"

"No, I'm just—"

"I'll wait for you upstairs, okay?"

"Sure. Here, take your camera."

She snatched it out of my hands and fled up the steps. I waited a
moment, then thudded up the stairs behind her. At the top, I found
her at a side door that led to the cloisters. The door was open and I
could see the green gardens outside. She was staring at something on
the wall.

"Desiree?"

"I'm sorry," she said. "Everyone always wants me to be such and
such a way, but I can't. I can only be me."

"I know," I said. "I'm okay with that."

I was still holding the lens cap of her camera and passed it to her.

"Wait," she said. "Let me get a photo of this thing."

"What thing?"

"Look," she said. Up between two pillars on a sort of shelf sat an odd
bronze sculpture. On a lectern in front of it was a description: LAMPADA
VOTIVA, it read. And underneath that: IL MIRACOLO DELL'AMORE. Even I
could understand that—the miracle of love.

"What's that supposed to be?" I asked.

The base was a banana-boat shape and above it, dangling on a
wire, was a circle with pointed spangly things sticking out of it.

"It's a votive lamp, for burning holy oil," she said.

"And that?" I asked, pointing to the thing on top. "Is that supposed to be a star?"

"It's the sun. It says on the plaque that the shape of the lamp represents the moon with the sun rising above it. Apparently, it's a Franciscan symbol."

"Friar Lawrence was a Franciscan," I said.

"It's a metaphor, right?" Desiree asked.

"It is," I said. "Juliet is the sun and Rosaline is the moon." It was as if Shakespeare himself had been in this cathedral—admiring the stars on the roof and this strange little votive lamp, the sun blotting out the moon, the old love gone pale in comparison to the real love that had eclipsed it.

"You think it's trying to tell us something?"

"You just smarten it up, mister," she said, then laughed. She snapped off a final photo and handed me the camera. I clipped on the lens cap and nestled it inside my daypack. She pulled me out the door, down a set of steps, out into the brilliant sunshine.

———

"You were going to tell me something," I said. "Yesterday. You stopped, but you were going to tell me something."

"Oh," she said.

We were walking back along the streets of Verona—on the other side of the river—where the bakers and mechanics live, where hardware stores and stationery shops line the streets.

"When I left Italy," she began, "I traveled all over the world."

"Okay."

"I surfed all over the world."

"Surf. Like in the ocean, surf?"

"Yeah," she said. "And the truth is, it's all I really want to do—just surf."

"That's it? That's what you wanted to tell me?"

217

She was struggling to explain something to me. I could see that.

"Out on the ocean," she said, "at dawn, with the sun just coming up, that's when I'm most myself."

"I love the water," I said. "I practically lived in the water when I was a kid."

"Really?" She brightened.

"I didn't know you were a surfer. I didn't see that coming."

"I surfed with Rafael," she said, "here in Italy. After that, I traveled all over: Sri Lanka, Fiji, Hawaii, Australia."

"What? By yourself?"

"Yes."

"That's brave."

"There's a fine line between bravery and stupidity. I was compet- ing then. I was pretty hard-core."

"Wow."

"So, all last year, you remember I was in Mexico, right?"

"Yeah."

"Yeah. I was training for another competition . . . and I got hurt."

"Ah shit, Desiree. Are you okay?"

"No, actually, not really. I was hurt quite badly. And that's when I finally came back to Canada," she said. "That was rock bottom, for me. Everything I tried . . ." She shrugged. "It felt like my life was over." She fixed me with a stare. "That's when I came to your place to pick up that book I lent you. That's where it comes full circle."

"I had no idea."

"And on your back deck," she said, "when you said you were going to Verona, I couldn't stop thinking about Italy again. I thought about it every day."

"And now, here you are."

"Yes. Here I am."

We were coming up to the Castelvecchio Bridge. The bricks were a rusty red, three arches spanning the lazy river. I felt for her hand and took it in mine, and we walked on in silence for a while. "It is kind of like fate," she said. "You have to admit that."

"What is?"

"That I got hurt. That I had to come back to Canada, right when all that stuff happened to you, with Claire. Everything fell into place for us to be here . . . together."

"I admit nothing."

"Come on," she said. "I'm serious."

The bridge opened up before us and we walked onto it. I was thinking about what she was saying. "Most of the research on love," I said, "talks about hormones and chemicals and biology."

"That's not very romantic."

"No, it's not. But it's true: We're hardwired for these biological drives. Certain patterns are set, and then they're very hard to break."

"Not romantic at all."

"Wait, I'm not finished. I think that—especially when we're young—we are slaves to these drives. It's biological destiny. That's a sort of fate, if you like."

"Yeah, maybe."

"But then you get older and you're not such—"

"Not such an idiot?" She squeezed my hand.

"You know what I mean. You don't have to do what your hormones are telling you to do. You can choose. You can defy the stars."

"I didn't choose to get hurt." She stopped and frowned at me. "That wasn't supposed to happen."

"No," I said.

"Not a very happy ending," she said.

"Maybe," I said, "maybe because that's not the ending."

We continued along the bridge, the swallowtail crenellations rising above us on both sides. "I guess," I said, "you could say that you did choose to come to Verona. I chose to come too."

"I guess," she said.

"Hey," I said, "we should go up onto the battlements. There's a good view of the Old City up there."

We clambered up a set of crumbling steps in the wall, up to an alcove overlooking the river. A breeze swept at Desiree's hair. Her face was as beautiful as the Venus in Botticelli's famous painting. We sat on the stones looking across the river at the spires and towers of old Verona. When I opened my daypack, thinking she might want her camera, she saw my notebook.

"Have you finished your letter yet?" she asked.

"Uh, no. Not really."

"Can I read it?"

"No," I said.

"Come on. Let me read it."

"Um . . ."

"Come on."

"Well . . ." I brought out the notebook and opened it up to the right page. "I only have the first paragraph." I handed it over and watched as her eyes trailed down the lines:

I despair of love, Juliet. I have been hurt many times and I am worn out and cynical. I am afraid of growing old alone.

Desiree already knew the whole story. I'd told it to her on my back deck. But even that seemed like a long time ago. When she finished reading, she stared at the paper. "It's beautiful," she said.

"It's pathetic," I said. "What I don't understand is why I had to go through all of that, you know, before I could come to my senses."

"I know," she said. "Why do you have to hit rock bottom before you can come up again?" She slipped the notebook back to me. "Are you going to finish the letter?"

"I don't know."

"I think you should post it, just as it is."

"Are you okay with that?"

"Why wouldn't I be?"

"Because it's about Claire."

"Is it really, though?"

"I don't . . . I mean, what? What do you mean?"

She considered me gravely. "Glenn, I don't want to grow old alone either."

"You said you didn't want to get married again."

"I don't. That's not the same thing. That's not what I'm saying."

"Okay, fair point."

We watched the world for a while. The late afternoon light was soft, silken almost.

"So," I said, "do you think you're going to be able to surf again?"

"Maybe," she said. "I'm healing, slowly."

I couldn't tell if she meant from the surfing or more than that.

"I think you will," I said. "I think you can do anything you set your mind to."

She turned to me. Her smile was incandescent. She leaned over then and kissed me. It was a warm kiss, delicate and very, very sweet. It was a kiss I will never forget.

"Hey," I said when she pulled away. "Does that kiss count?"

"Yes," she said. "That one counts."

———

That evening, under the towering medieval city walls, Desiree and I dined at the Pizzeria Leon d'Oro. The waiters bustled in and out from the kitchen in the old manor house behind us. The evening was warm. Desiree sat across from me, the soft lamplight gentle on her face. Above us, the stars had come out over the ancient walls. I could see the belt of Orion, tipping up to the east.

We'd walked all day. I'd dragged along my daypack and it sat at my feet. Between us, on the table, was a bottle of Valpolicella Classico

Allegrini. We'd ordered our pizzas—a *capricciosa* pizza for me, a *margherita* for her.

"This really is a fantastic place," I said.

Desiree's eyes twinkled. "I love it," she answered.

I took a sip of the ruby-red wine.

The waiter arrived with our pizzas. The mozzarella was light and the artichokes smelled rich and earthy. Desiree lifted a piece from her plate and folded it over on itself. She brought it to her mouth, seemed to think of something, and put it down again.

"Thanks," she said.

"For what?"

"I like myself better when I'm with you, that's all."

"Me too," I said. "I love being with you."

She stared down at her plate. "I need to ask you something."

"Okay."

"I need to ask you: What happens next?"

"Well, I thought we were going to travel around Italy a bit."

"Yeah, no . . . not that. We will. I have some friends I want to see. I mean, after that."

She held my gaze. She looked beautiful and I thought that, yes, I wanted to spend a whole lot more time with her.

Her fingers fumbled up to her locket. "I need to go back to the ocean," she said, "just like I needed to come to Italy. Do you know what I mean?" She paused. "I was kind of hoping you'd come with me."

"Go with you to a tropical paradise?" I smiled. "Yeah, I think I could manage that."

She laughed. "Oh," she said, "I do like you so."

After dinner, we walked back to Emiliano's under a sky full of stars. We walked hand in hand, and that night—I guess I don't have to tell you—we moved our things into just one of the bedrooms. This time we really did meet at the Gates of Paradise, and in the morning

I woke with her beside me, feeling happy, perfectly in accord with the universe.

———

On the morning of Juliet's 730th birthday, Desiree needed some extra time to get ready for the big day, so I tramped up the streets to the Piazza delle Erbe by myself. The fruit stalls were already open, and the fountain was splashing with water. A little farther on, I ducked through a passageway that led into the Piazza dei Signori. The piazza is surrounded by some of the oldest and most beautiful buildings in Verona, and in the center of the cobblestone square, rising up on a white marble pedestal, stands a statue of Dante Alighieri himself. The palace of the Scala family takes up one side of the piazza, and I knew that somewhere in the rooms behind that ornate facade, a very real Prince Escalus had told Dante the story of love and loss that had oc-curred in his city.

When I entered the piazza, I saw Jolyon and Manuela coming from the other direction. Jolyon had a tape recorder in a satchel over his shoulder. In his right hand he held a microphone with a large furry windbreak. He wore a ball cap, and over that a set of head-phones. He was listening intently, holding up the mic in various di-rections. Manuela walked beside him, explaining, gesturing with her hands at the magnificent buildings all around.

"Buon giorno," she called when she saw me.

"Hi," I said. "I wanted to see where we'd be reading our letters," I began. "It's beautiful here."

"Oh," said Manuela, "but it will not be exactly here."

"No? I thought—"

"There is a smaller square, even more lovely." She stopped. Jolyon lowered his microphone. "Come," she said. "Please, you can follow me."

We trailed after her through a smaller passageway between two buildings. The narrow alley ran off to the left and we ducked through it into a much smaller square. High above us rose a medieval bell tower.

"Here," said Manuela, "is the Torre dei Lamberti."

We craned our necks up. The tower rose like a square chimney of pale red bricks. At the top, high above us, a shining white cupola stabbed into the blue sky.

"The Lamberti Tower was begun in 1140. It is the tallest tower in Verona," said Manuela.

"Brilliant," said Jolyon.

"Now, please," said Manuela, "you will look at the stairs leading up to the entrance."

We both turned.

If heaven had a staircase, it would be modeled after this one. A soft pink balustrade angled up the side of the building, its limestone buttresses glowing like the inside of a seashell. The steps rose steeply, then turned ninety degrees at a landing and continued up another flight to the tower entrance. The arches were supported by fluted columns, and in the stone pediments above the columns were faces carved into the stone, peering down like peasants in a Brueghel painting.

"Wow," I said.

"It is here," said Manuela, "that we will read the letters. This is called Scala della Ragione—the Stairs of Reason."

———

Desiree and I had agreed to meet at Juliet's house, but when I arrived, the crowds were bunching up at the tunnel leading into the courtyard. I saw Desiree searching for me, bobbing in the river of people. She wore a white, Gypsy-style shirt and a long blue-gray peasant skirt. Her hair shone golden and my heart gave a little lurch.

I waded through the throng to her. "Wow, you look dazzling."

"Thanks," she said, over the noise of the bustling crowd. "What's going on?"

"It's starting."

"I just saw Anna go by," she said. "She's already inside."

"Quick, then. Through the sewing shop," I said.

"Who are you? James Bond?" She grabbed my hand and we swung into the sewing shop door, past the displays of heart-shaped cushions and monogrammed tea towels. An older lady, her white hair in a tight bun, worked at a sewing machine near the back. She didn't even look up as we flashed by. The back door let us out beside the red letter box in the corner of the courtyard; across the cobblestones, a semicircle of people had formed under Juliet's balcony.

Anna stood on a step near the entrance to the house, a microphone in her hand. She was reading from a piece of paper, welcoming the crowd. Near the front of the semicircle, I could see Jolyon, his bald head still shielded under the ball cap, his big, bug-like headphones pulled down over his ears. Soňa had muscled her way to the front too and was standing near Anna.

And under the balcony, in the clearing, stood Romeo. Or, at least, a young man dressed as Romeo. He wore a dark purple shirt with white puffy sleeves, and he had a red velvet cape carelessly slung over his shoulder. His pantaloons ballooned at his thighs but tapered down into knee-high leather boots. He was about eighteen, square-jawed, and handsome, Italian handsome, his hair pomaded into a swaggering wave above his forehead.

Desiree and I stayed at the back door of the shop as Anna clicked on a ghetto blaster. A swell of orchestral music filled the courtyard and the crowd hushed. Our young Romeo strode back and forth on the bare cobblestones, looking pensively up at the balcony above him.

"Here it comes," I said.

Juliet emerged onto the balcony high above the crowds, leaning wistfully, just like the graphic on the envelopes. She was young and beautiful, wearing a pale dress the color of the sky. Her sleeves billowed out and a strand of her dark hair was braided around her head, like a tiara. She leaned her cheek on her hand. "Oh Romeo, Romeo," she called and the crowd below the balcony went perfectly still. *"Perchè sei tu Romeo."*

"It's in Italian," I said. "And they skipped some bits," I said.

"Glenn, shhh!"

The actors played out the scene until the moment when Romeo is supposed to climb up and kiss her. I don't think they'd thought this through, because they both paused then, each waiting for the other to do something. Then Romeo unfurled his cape, improvising, and he pushed through the crowd, making a break for the front entrance to Juliet's house. He swept past Anna and disappeared inside. Anna began to applaud, and the crowd picked up her cue. That seemed to be the end of the first event of the day, though none of this was on Barbara's agenda.

"You know," I said, "I can't quite imagine it."

"Imagine what?" Desiree asked.

"What it was like here seven hundred years ago."

"Well, it is probably her house. We know that."

"Yes, but the play says Romeo climbed the wall and came down into a garden. I don't see any garden."

"You're taking it too literally," said Desiree.

Anna began ushering people out the archway. She saw us and waved just before she herself disappeared under it. The crowds funneled out behind her.

"No one can really know what happened here," said Desiree.

"True."

"If there was a Romeo and Juliet," she said, "I mean a real Romeo and Juliet, then they're the only ones who knew what actually took place."

"There probably wasn't a balcony."

"Maybe not, but it makes for a better story."

She was right, of course. "I guess," I said. "I just want to believe that the main points are still true—that true love existed here, a love strong enough to defeat a centuries-old hatred."

We both considered the ancient courtyard for a moment. It had largely emptied of people, and the old house rose up before us. The chalk-red bricks were weathered with age, and in a window to the right of the balcony, a face peered down at us, largely obscured by the dark glass. Then it retreated into the shadows and I took in a breath.

"What?" Desiree asked.

"Nothing," I said. "Maybe we should head for the piazza. The show will be starting soon."

———

The reading of the letters was to begin at three o'clock. Desiree and I strolled through the Piazza delle Erbe, past the Roman statue and the fountain. We veered right, through the market stalls, in between two buildings, the archway above them hung with the rib of a whale.

"Where are we going?" Desiree asked.

"The Piazza dei Signori. Through here," I said. "This is where we're reading the letters."

We ducked through the passage into the square. Climbing up along the wall to our right was the Scala della Ragione. The Lamberti Tower loomed above everything and I could see why they'd decided on three o'clock. The sun was behind the tower, and the shadows now were deep and cool.

Barbara stood behind a folding table. She was arranging stacks of postcards. She smiled at us almost wistfully. Everything would either come together now or it wouldn't, and there was nothing more she could do. They'd set up a plywood podium painted to look like Juliet's balcony. A boom microphone was set up, and everything looked ready to go.

In the shadow of the highest arch under the stairs, the actors mingled, speaking with one another in a tight circle, though my actor, the Oktoberfest man, stroked his beard and paced back and forth, rehearsing his lines. I checked my watch. It was half past two. The crowd was growing in the square. Manuela plodded through the passageway with Jolyon. The oversize furry microphone was still in his hand but his headphones hung around his neck.

"Where's your letter?" Desiree asked.

"My letter?"

"The one you have to read. Didn't you say it needed some editing?"

I pulled it from my back pocket and passed it to Desiree. At the table where Barbara had been standing, there was an empty chair. Desiree sat and smoothed the letter in front of her. She reached for a pen.

Jolyon sidled in beside me. "Everything ready?" he asked.

"I hope so."

"You know, they gave me some letters to answer."

I waited for him to go on.

"Bloody difficult," he said.

"I know."

"I told Anna that under no circumstances should anyone take relationship advice from me."

"I felt pretty much the same way when I started."

"Listen," he said, reaching into his satchel, "would you mind terribly if I asked you a few questions, for Radio Four?" He yanked the headphones onto his ears again and gave me a warning look, like I should prepare myself. He dug in his satchel and flicked a switch, and a tiny red light popped on before I had a chance to say no.

"On the day of Juliet's birthday," he began, "I met Glenn Dixon, who appeared to be the only man answering letters." He turned to face me, the microphone hovering between us. "Do you think you answer the letters differently because you're male?"

"Oh," I said. I should have known this question was coming. "I think that everyone feels pretty much the same thing when it comes to love. Most of the letters are from young women, that's true, but the ones I saw from men, they weren't really that different."

"But don't you feel compelled to dole out advice? Isn't that supposed to be the male tendency?"

"Sometimes," I said. "I talk with the other secretaries about how to answer. Sometimes you really want to tell these people to get it together, to smarten up—but of course you can't say that. That's not what they want to hear."

"And what do they want to hear?" Jolyon lifted a hand to his headphones.

"Mostly, they just want to tell their stories, to be listened to. They write because they still want to believe in love, you know? They want to believe in Juliet."

"I would imagine that everyone wants to believe in true love."

"One of the secretaries once told me that every time I answer a letter, I'm really answering myself."

Jolyon raised his eyebrows. "And what do you tell yourself?"

"Maybe," I said, "that you can choose to be happy. Maybe that what you need to do is love yourself first. Then, I guess, others can follow your example." I paused. "Another secretary told me that one."

I heard my name being called. Jolyon grimaced and flicked off the tape recorder. "I think you're wanted," he said.

I wish now that I'd had more time to respond but, really, it would take a whole book to answer the questions of love. What is the elusive cure for heartbreak and why do we cling so fervently to the objects of our desire? Well, they say that when one door closes, another will open, but I don't think that's strictly true. The secret is to open yourself up, to open yourself to entirely new possibilities. For thousands of years people believed that the sun circled around the earth—because that's what it looked like. The sun rose in the east and arced across the sky. Only it doesn't. The sun doesn't move at all. And it takes that kind of Copernican shift to see what is truly real.

It's we who are caught in the gravitational pull of love. But it's also up to us to know how to deal with it, to know when to leap off and when to fly.

"Glenn!"

Barbara was waving at me from the fake balcony. She had the others lined up behind her like they were about to be chosen for a team on sports day. Desiree was in the middle. She too was waving at me to hurry over.

Giovanna and her father stood to the side, under the stairwell. Giulio wasn't wearing a tie, just a dark blue sweater vest over a collared shirt. He tipped his head at me as I rushed past. I took that as a note of encouragement.

I reached Desiree. "It's boy, girl, boy, girl," she said. "You're going first."

"First? Why me?"

"Because you're a boy. Go!" She gave me a gentle shove to the front of the line. "Wait," she said. "Your letter." She handed me her edits, scribbled quickly on the page. "Sorry," she said. "It's the best I could do." She smiled and squeezed my arm. *"In bocca al lupo,"* she said.

"What does that mean?"

"Literally, 'in the mouth of the wolf.'"

"What?"

"It means good luck." She laughed.

The actors had gathered under the landing. By the stairs, Manuela's daughter, the ballerina, was warming up, her slippered foot on a step, her arm sweeping gracefully over it in a slow arc. I raced past her to take my place in line just in front of Soňa. "Hey, where are your glasses?" I asked Soňa.

"I don't like to wear them in public," she said. "People say I look like Katniss without them—you know, from *The Hunger Games.*"

"You do."

She smiled at that. I could picture her with a bow and arrow, some kind of deadly ninja cupid.

Anna swept down the row, chirping a good luck to everyone.

"Oh, look," Soňa said. "There's Veronica." Veronica had come in through the passageway. She waved at us. Near her, still in costume, were the two young actors who had played Romeo and Juliet.

"Quite a circus," I said. "So much going on."

"It's Juliet's birthday. Of course there's a lot going on."

Barbara stepped to the microphone. She spoke bravely, confidently, and then she turned to check that I was still behind her. She leaned into the microphone. *"Inglese,"* she said, and then stepped away.

The bare podium beckoned. I lurched forward and the microphone gave a squeal of feedback. I held out my letter. Desiree had penned a lot of edits. I should have looked it over first, but I hadn't had time.

"'Dear Juliet,'" I began. My voice echoed around the square—my voice and yet not my voice anymore. "'I am a thirty-four-year-old man from Helsinki,'" I read, "'and I am in love with my sweetheart.'" Desiree had fixed the spelling from *sweet hard* to *sweetheart.* "'My love is as strong as a mountain.'" Good God, who writes this crap? Maybe it sounded better in Finnish. "'I like to see her smile,'" I read. "'She is the most beautiful woman in the world. Her eyes melt me like butter. Her touch is like a thousand feathers on my chest. Please let me hold this forever.'" I looked for more, but that was the full letter. I nodded to the Oktoberfest man, who started in on the Italian translation. His voice boomed across the square. He finished and stepped back proudly from the microphone. I shuffled to the end of the line. Desiree smiled as I passed her. "That was great," she said.

"Czech," Barbara said into the microphone. Soňa plodded forward. *"Drahá Julie,'"* she began. When she finished, Stefano came forward—a young man who looked nervous, his hands shaking. He read out the Russian letter, his voice becoming stronger as he went.

Finally, it was Desiree's turn. She strode to the microphone. Barbara watched like a proud mother.

"'Dear Juliet,'" Desiree began in English. Her peasant blouse was a brilliant white. So were her watch strap and the bracelet on her right hand. She was luminescent.

"'I am twenty-six years old, and I have had terrible luck when it comes to love and romance. After four years, my high school sweetheart called off our wedding and left without any explanation.'" Desiree paused.

"'I would have done anything for him,'" she continued. "'I spent many nights crying myself to sleep, wondering if there was something wrong with me. After that, I decided to change my life and focus on myself. I moved into a new house, bought a new car, and joined the town council. I went on holidays and used the time to find out who I really am. I am happy and independent now, but I still want to find love. The truth is, Juliet, I want true love so badly that my heart hurts.'"

She looked up, her eyes searching the crowd until they found mine. "'So Juliet,'" Desiree finished, "'whatever influence you might have in the universe, put in a good word for me, because my hope is fading and my heart hurts. Love, April.'"

Desiree rushed around to stand beside me. I felt for her hand and took it in mine. More letters followed. German and French, and then Manuela read the Japanese letter, which resonated with all the same dreams as the ones before it. Love, I thought, truly is universal—its hopes, its joys, its sorrows.

After the letters, Desiree and I moved out into the crowd, now four or five people deep. I wanted to see what Gloria, Anna's artist friend, was working on, so we edged our way to the entrance of the grand staircase. Gloria stood in front of an easel, her back to the crowd, but the painting before her was entirely black.

"I don't get it," I said to Desiree.

"Just wait," she answered.

Gloria held a tin can in one hand. She dabbed at it with a paintbrush and applied a liquid to the blackness, but there was nothing to see except a sheen, like water, something wet and clear and shiny. She gave a few more dabs, then knelt down to the cobblestones, reaching into a box at her feet. She drew a fine red powder up in both hands, cupping it like snow before tossing it at the canvas. From the cloud of dust, an image exploded—Juliet's statue, the head turned demurely, one hand raised, the other lost in the furls of her diaphanous gown.

"Wow," I said. "It's Juliet."

"It is," said Desiree. "It is."

Manuela's daughter, Lucrezia, danced next. She pirouetted with a letter, holding it out at arm's length as if to read it.

Desiree leaned into me. "She's really good," she said.

Barbara pushed toward us. She said something in staccato Italian. "You're up next, Glenn," Desiree said. "You're the final act."

"The Shakespeare reading?"

"*Sì,*" said Barbara. "Shakespeare, Shakespeare."

Manuela's daughter finished her dance by sinking gracefully to the cobblestones. She stood up and a great boom of applause thundered through the square. At the far edge of the square, the purple-caped Romeo was staring at me. The young actress playing Juliet stood beside him.

"Go," said Desiree. "You're on."

I stepped to the podium. The crowd stilled. Romeo struck a pose in front of me. What was he meant to do? he seemed to be asking.

"*But soft,*" I began. "*What light through yonder window breaks?*"

Juliet climbed the staircase behind me. Her face peeked down from a balustrade above.

It is the east, and Juliet is the sun.
Arise, fair sun and kill the envious moon.

I saw Desiree, her hand on her locket, her eyes fixed on me. Romeo threw up his arm as if he were saying the lines himself, and I remembered my students, Sadia especially, rapt at this scene. I remembered Devin kicking at his desk leg, but listening, always listening.

"*I am too bold,*" I continued. "*'Tis not to me she speaks.*"

Romeo lingered at the steps. Above him, Juliet sighed and rested a white cheek on her hand.

The crowd was entranced. Could I really do the lines justice? I took a breath and barreled on. "*Two of the fairest stars in all the heaven, having some business, do entreat her eyes to twinkle in their spheres till they return.*" The Shakespeare tumbled off my tongue as only Shakespeare can. I'd seen these very lines in the old quarto. A mad king had marked them as special. "*The brightness of her cheek would shame those stars as daylight doth a lamp. Her eyes in heaven would through the airy region stream so bright that birds would sing and think it were not night.*"

"*Ay me,*" said Juliet from above.

"*O speak again, bright angel.*"

Behind me, Romeo raced up the stairs toward his Juliet. "*As glorious to this night, being over my head,*" I continued, "*as is a winged messenger of heaven unto the white-upturned wondering eyes of mortals.*"

I let those last few words hang in the air for a moment. Above me, Romeo had reached Juliet, and they embraced. All was still. I took a little bow and a smattering of applause rippled through the square, growing in volume until it became a sustained roar. I heard a few bravos, and I bowed again just before Barbara charged in to take the microphone from me. And then, that was it. Barbara said some closing remarks. Romeo and Juliet vanished. And Juliet's birthday was over.

———

Once the square had cleared, Barbara dipped into the alcove under the stairs and returned with a couple of bottles of red wine. Giovanna swept in behind her with a couple of more whites. Giulio worked the corkscrew and passed the open bottles around. We filled our plastic cups, pouring for one another, the secretaries and actors and volunteers. Barbara was jubilant. We hoisted our cups in a toast to her. Giulio marched over to stand behind Desiree and me. He put a hand on her shoulder and said something to her. Then I felt his other hand come to rest on my shoulder. He held it there for a moment, though he never looked at me. His speech was short and in Italian. Still, I understood that he was pleased with the celebrations, and his hand on my shoulder was the single greatest compliment I received that day.

Giovanna looked more at ease than I'd ever seen her. She caught my eye and stepped in toward us. "You will be leaving Verona now?" she asked.

"Yes, I think so. Probably tomorrow," I said.

"Then I wish to thank you both for your time here. You have been a great help."

"Thanks," I said. "It was our pleasure."

"And you," she said to Desiree. They broke into Italian, standing together as if they'd known each other for years. I took a step backward and bumped into someone behind me. Anna had slipped in tentatively, waiting to speak with me.

"You are leaving?" she asked.

"Probably tomorrow," I said. "We want to see more of Italy."

"It's a very beautiful country."

"What will you do now?" I asked.

"I don't know. I would like to work for a nonprofit."

"Ah," I said. "You will save the world."

"Probably," she said, brightening. "Probably I would like that."

Someone called her name and she whirled off with a smile. Then Jolyon emerged from the crowd. He sidled up beside me, tucking his microphone away.

"Did you get everything you needed?" I asked.

"More than enough," he said. "I'd like to air it on Valentine's Day."

"That's a ways off."

"Yes, but that's not unusual. It takes some time to edit these things."

Desiree skipped over to us with her camera.

"Would you like me to take a photo, just the two of you?" asked Jolyon.

"Yes, please," she said, passing him her camera.

"What if," he said, "you go up there?" He gestured up the staircase to the balcony at the very top.

"Is that all right?" I asked Desiree, but she was already pulling me to the stairs. I felt strange walking up those steps, as if only princes and poets were allowed to ascend. We rose, up and up, climbing to the top where a sort of balcony jutted out in front of the thick oaken doors of the tower. The doors were set in an arch framed by pillars of spiraling white marble. Above it, in the tympanum, an ancient fresco called the Allegory of Verona was still visible. A muse, or an angel maybe, sat in Roman dress with a book open on her lap as if she had just finished reading it. We walked to the balustrade and leaned over the railing. Far below us in the square, Jolyon motioned for us to step a little to the left. I put my arm around Desiree. Before us lay the gleaming rooftops of old Verona, shining in the last of the afternoon sun.

Jolyon raised the camera and snapped a few shots. Desiree mouthed a thank-you down to him. He nodded and then went to speak to others in the crowd. Desiree and I were silent for a moment; then she turned to me as if she'd just remembered something. "Did you post your letter yet?"

"No," I said. "But I don't think I will."

A clear blue sky was reflected in her eyes.

"Why?" she asked.

"Because," I said, pulling her toward me. "I've already got my answer."

Epilogue

The epiphany of love

I jogged barefoot along the beach, a long, white stretch of sand ahead of me. The waves frothed and lapped up to my feet, but I plugged along, loping really, dodging the silver surf when it washed too high. I didn't run very far, just out to a rocky point where a dog pranced along the shore with a stick in his mouth. He was the only other living thing I'd seen except for the seaweed. I turned back, my footprints collapsing behind me in the sand. I'd left a towel and a water bottle in the shade of a palm tree, but when I returned the sun had found them.

It had been more than a year since we'd left Verona. I sat on a fallen tree at the edge of the beach and watched a pelican swoop along the crest of the waves. The sea was an emerald green, breaking just out from the shoreline, thumping and washing up the sand in a bubbling froth.

Desiree was standing in the water. She must have surfed her last wave all the way into shore, dropping to paddle the last few feet. She undid the leash from her ankle, and tucked her surfboard under her arm. Her wet hair hung down her back. She waved at me.

"You looked great out there," I called.

She cupped an ear to tell me she couldn't hear me over the surf and strode up the sand toward me.

"I saw a turtle!" she said when she arrived. "It popped its head out. It looked right at me."

"Cool," I said.

She laid her surfboard down in the shade, fins up, and gave a little shiver. I wrapped my beach towel around her shoulders.

"I love it here," she said.

"Just think. It's the middle of winter back home," I said. "The kids are back in school." I could still picture it so clearly, the fluorescent lights buzzing, the rustle of books being opened.

"Do you miss it?" she asked. "Do you miss being a teacher?"

"Here," I said, "let's sit in the sun. We walked down a little closer to the waterline, and she laid the towel down on the sand.

"I don't really miss the teaching," I said. "All the planning, all the marking. I don't miss that at all. But I think about my students a lot. I wonder how they're doing."

"You made a difference in their lives. You know that, right?"

"I hope so."

My former students would be out in the real world now. Sadia was probably in a university lecture hall, sitting in the front row. Devin, wherever he was, would be causing problems. Allison would be in law school, and maybe she was still with Andy. Minh's English was probably pretty good by now, and Marc, well, I hoped he'd found his way. Over the years, probably three thousand students had passed through my classroom, and I did wonder what had become of them all.

We'd heard from Giovanna that the Club di Giulietta had opened another new office in Verona. Giulio, I think, had decided to close down the old one on the Via Galilei. That building had served its purpose. Thousands of letters and thousands of stories had passed through its doors. The secretaries had answered them all with good counsel, patience, and grace. Giovanna e-mailed me when she heard I was writing a book about my time as a secretary to Juliet. "I am happy for your good fortune," she said, and she asked when Desiree and I might visit again.

In the spring, Soňa had traveled all the way to Canada to visit us. We took her to the mountains and she bought a snowy owl keepsake in Banff. Anna returned to university to study for a master's degree in fund-raising. I was proud of her for that. Manuela was leading tours across the Old City, teaching people about Dante and his connection to Romeo and Juliet. At Juliet's house, the right breast on her statue would be polished to an even thinner eggshell of gold, though her expression, demure and distant and just a little bit sad, would never change.

"Earth to Glenn," said Desiree. She'd nestled into me on the towel. "Where art thou?"

"I was just thinking about Verona," I said. "Sometimes, I can't believe everything that's happened. I mean, look at this. Everything has turned out so perfectly."

"That's right, Mr. Destiny." She kissed my cheek.

"I'm serious. I can't help but wonder, what was I supposed to learn from all this?"

"And what do you suppose you've learned?" she asked.

"That I don't ever want to feel heartache again. That I don't ever want to be jealous or hopeless or sad. And"—I met her eyes—"that I want to be with you. You're the best thing that's ever happened to me, Desiree."

She smiled and leaned into me.

"What about you?" I asked. "What have you learned?"

"Me?" She paused. "Well, it's as if the dust has been swept from my path and now it's clear. Now I know where to walk." She tucked her head into my shoulder. "And I'll walk it with you."

"That's a pretty good answer," I said.

Far on the horizon, a ship was sailing away. It was too distant to tell whether it was a cruise ship or a cargo container, just a dot on the ocean headed for faraway lands.

Right at that moment, I knew I didn't want to be anywhere else in the world. There was no pain in my heart. No uncertainty. There was me. There was Desiree. And that was all I needed. I am no longer young. I know that. But I know who I am. I'm no longer at the mercy of the tides of my youth. And I know that I'm happy.

I remember one piece of research from among the hundreds of papers and books that I read about love. It was just a little aside, quite unrelated to the hard data of the research paper. Most of the world's love stories, it said, are not love stories at all; rather, they are the stories of courtship, of those magical days at the beginning. There's much less written about the long years that follow, about growing old together, about love that lasts and lasts and lasts. And isn't that what true love is really all about?

Four hundred years ago, Shakespeare wrote something much the same.

"*Love's not Time's fool,*" he wrote.

Love alters not with his brief hours and weeks,
But bears it out even to the edge of doom.
If this be error and upon me proved,
I never writ, nor no man ever loved.

A Walking Tour of Old Verona

The following tour correlates to the map on pages 244 and 245.

The cobblestoned streets and shaded alleys of Verona are well-worn by those who have walked them over the millennia. Roman legions, star-crossed teenagers, and lovelorn authors have all followed these twisting paths through the heart of the ancient city, leaving their own indelible marks for the next travelers to find. What will you discover in Verona?

As Glenn learned, every journey must start from the heart. Roman engineers first laid out the heart of Verona within a bend of the Adige River, and the generations that came afterward turned the Old City into a dense cluster of *piazzas* and *corsos*. Consider beginning your walk in the **Piazza delle Erbe (1)**, the old vegetable market. Here, you can haggle over fresh fennel and honey from the Veneto countryside and enjoy a glass of amarone in the shadow of the **Torre dei Lamberti (2)**. The 276-foot spire was constructed in the twelfth century and has watched over Verona ever since—its bell may very well have tolled out the deaths of Romeo and Juliet. A spectacular view from the top awaits explorers who brave the stairs, though a lift will take you there all the same. Stepping out of the piazza, you are only a short walk from the **Casa di Giulietta (3)**, out of which so much of Glenn's story unfolds. Perhaps you're there for a quick kiss on the balcony. Or maybe you're delivering a letter of your own.

Then consider strolling through the **Vicolo Santa Cecilia (4)**, a narrow street almost untouched by time, where the new office of the Club di Giulietta lies hidden, to the beautiful **Tomba di Cangrande della Scala (5)**. Here, the remains of Prince Escalus are interred within the walls of the church of Santa Maria Antica, along with four other elegant tombs of Veronese rulers. Just around the corner sits the **"Casa di Romeo" (6)**. Although it may not be the true seat of the Montague family, this proud fourteenth-century fortification sits resplendent with dovetail crenellations, and is well worth the short walk.

Following the Adige south from the **Ponte Nuovo (7)**, you can wend your way along the riverbank to the ruins of the monastery of San Francesco al Corso, under which the **Tomba di Giulietta (8)** has survived the centuries. Perhaps you will be fortunate, as Glenn was, to enjoy a quiet moment in the stillness of the crypt. A bust of Shakespeare at the entrance to the tomb watches over the young woman to whom he gave immortality—be sure to read the words on the faded bronze plaque beside it. Tucked behind the monastery is the small *pensione* where Glenn stayed, at number 7, **Via dei Montecchi (9)**. Is this the true home of the Montague family? Verona still holds its secrets.

If you have come this far, the day may very well be winding down. There is no place better to dine in Verona than the centuries-old **Pizzeria Leon d'Oro (10)**, just a few blocks away from the Via dei Montecchi. Here, Glenn and Desiree shared a bottle of Valpolicella Classico Allegrini and began to contemplate a life together. After dinner, a short walk east will take you to the **Arena di Verona (11)**. Constructed nearly two thousand years ago, it is one of the best-preserved Roman buildings in the world. The arena is breathtaking enough during the day, but nothing short of spectacular at night. Attend the opera, as Glenn did, if you can. If not, you can always swing by the world-renowned **Gelateria Savoia (12)** nearby, and take in the majesty of the ancient architecture with an unforgettable gelato in hand.

Beyond the arena, against the western arm of the Adige, sits the **Castelvecchio (13)**, with its rust-red bricks, though this may be a journey for another day. From these imposing walls, the princes of Verona ruled their swath of northern Italy for centuries. Farther afield is the **Basilica di San Zeno Maggiore (14)**, under whose vaulted arches Romeo and Juliet married in secret.

A Walking Tour of Old Verona

There are discoveries beyond counting to be made in Verona. Many are built of brick and mortar, but still more are found within our hearts and minds. When we step out of our normal lives, as Glenn and Desiree and so many others have, into this city, we cannot help but discover something about ourselves in the journey.

What will you bring back with you when you return?

Acknowledgments

At some point, I knew I wasn't writing this book anymore. This book was writing me. No one could have been more surprised when Desiree came along in the middle of it. Desiree, you are the love I've been waiting for all my life. Thank you, thank you, my surfer girl, you are the best thing that's ever happened to me.

As for the secretaries of Juliet, I give you my heartfelt respect and gratitude. You are a most remarkable group of people, without fail welcoming and compassionate. I want to especially thank Giovanna Tamassia and her father, Giulio, who really are the essence of the Club di Giulietta. Your devotion to the letters is nothing short of inspirational. Anna and Soňa and Veronica, you are my friends for life, and I thank you for your good humor and companionship. There are others I didn't have a chance to mention in the pages of this book, and I want to thank you too. All of you made my travels to Italy extraordinary. I want to also say to the reader that, should you ever travel to Verona, Manuela Uber is a first-class guide to the city with a depth of knowledge that goes well beyond the information presented in this book.

All the letters I have quoted from were real, although I have changed all the names and locations. I want to honor all those who write to Juliet— some ten thousand a year now—and I hope that each of you finds, as I did, the answers you are seeking.

I did teach for twenty-one years and I'm quite sure I taught *Romeo and Juliet* every one of those years. The students in these pages are composites drawn from the thousands of students I taught over the decades. To all my real Sadias and Andys and Devins and their classmates—this is not you in

Acknowledgments

these pages. You and your many classmates may have misbehaved, you may have challenged me, and certainly you made me laugh, but I assure you, this is not any of you. I can say, though, that I have represented my classroom as truly as I possibly could and that it was a pleasure to relive it in the writing.

For Claire, I wish you real happiness in the life you have chosen. I know you will be a wonderful mother.

The final form of this book would not have been possible without the help and vision of my literary agent, Hilary McMahon. She worked with me for well over a year on the structure of this book. In fact, she kept phoning me while I was working through the initial draft to get the latest updates on what was happening—the two of us in constant disbelief about how the events were unfolding.

Likewise, I want to recognize the brilliant sensibilities of my Canadian editor, Nita Pronovost, as well as Abby Zidle, my American editor, both at Simon & Schuster. We went through this manuscript so many times I lost count, but every time it did get a little bit better. The entire staff at Simon & Schuster have been exceptional. There was an infectious excitement about this project right from the beginning that kept me going through the long hours and countless drafts.

Last, I wish to thank the Alberta Foundation for the Arts for their financial support as well as the generous encouragement of my friends and fellow writers at the Writers' Union of Canada, the Writers' Guild of Alberta, and the Creative Nonfiction Collective. To paraphrase Shakespeare: I have been at a great feast of languages, and stolen the scraps.

About the Author

David Whyte, Griffin Pictures

An author, musician, and documentary filmmaker, Glenn Dixon has traveled through more than seventy-five countries and written for *National Geographic*, the *New York Post*, *The Walrus*, *The Globe and Mail*, and *Psychology Today*. He holds an MA in sociolinguistics, and his second book, *Tripping the World Fantastic*, was short-listed for the W. O. Mitchell Literary Prize. A high school English teacher for more than twenty years, he has left that to become a full-time writer. Visit him at **GlennDixon.ca** or follow him on Twitter **@Glenn_Dixon**.

Juliet's Answer

GLENN DIXON

This reading group guide for Juliet's Answer includes an introduction, discussion questions, ideas for enhancing your book club, and a Q&A with author Glenn Dixon. The suggested questions are intended to help your reading group find new and interesting angles and topics for your discussion. We hope that these ideas will enrich your conversation and increase your enjoyment of the book. Just be aware that this material may contain spoilers!

Introduction

A lovelorn, seemingly "star-cross'd" English teacher takes the trip of a life-time to heal a broken heart and better understand the nature of love in this charming memoir that is part *Eat Pray Love*, part *Under the Tuscan Sun*, and part Shakespeare.

> *In fair Verona where we lay our scene . . .*

After his long-burning love for a friend goes unrequited for the last time, and in spectacularly dramatic fashion, Glenn Dixon seeks a new perspective on love in the most hallowed setting imaginable: Verona, Italy. A longtime English teacher, Dixon hopes that the setting and historical context of Shakespeare's classic *Romeo and Juliet* will help him untangle his own feelings. While in Verona, Dixon joins the Secretaries of Juliet, a group dedicated to answering each and every one of the love letters from around the world addressed to Juliet. His new, temporary role helps him cope with his own heartbreak while learning that love is an all-powerful force no matter the language or the place.

While in Verona, Glenn also surveys the historical and cultural impact of *Romeo and Juliet*. Is their story in fact true? How and why did Shakespeare fictionalize aspects of it? How does this midsize city handle all the tourism—and heartache? Upon his return, Glenn brings the story to life in the classroom, trying to impart the power of love and the brilliance of Shakespeare to his students.

Juliet's Answer is a highly personal and historical chronicle of love for the modern age.

Topics and Questions for Discussion

1. What was your reaction to learning that there is an enterprise be-hind answering letters to Juliet? Is there a responsibility to answer the letters?

2. Do you think that seeking advice from a semifictional character from a romantic tragedy is either romantic or tragic?

3. Is there a common trait shared by the secretaries? Do you think you could manage to be one of them?

4. What has your experience with reading Shakespeare been like throughout your life? Do you think you read and appreciate him differently as an adult than you did as an adolescent? Why or why not?

5. Can you think of any other literary settings so uniquely tied to their books and characters as Verona in *Romeo and Juliet*? Have you or would you ever visit any of them?

6. How would you characterize Glenn's teaching style? Does he remind you of any teacher you had during your school years?

7. Were there any new revelations for you about Shakespeare and/or *Romeo and Juliet*?

8. Describe Glenn and Claire's relationship. Are they wrong in how they treat each other? How would you describe Glenn's reaction to Claire's big reveal?

9. Has the digital age changed how we experience love? If so, do you think it's for better or for worse? If not, then explain your reasoning.

10. Have you ever taken a trip to heal yourself? Was it cathartic? Do you think that going on an adventure to somewhere new and different helps us learn and heal?

11. What role do you think timing had to play in Glenn and Desiree's budding relationship? Do you think that "timing is everything," acts as a principal factor in all relationships?

12. How do Glenn and Desiree complement each other? What type of future do you envision for them?

Enhance Your Book Club

1. A knowledge of Shakespeare's play is helpful in reading and understanding this book. Watch a production of *Romeo and Juliet*, be it on-screen or onstage, before discussing *Juliet's Answer*.

2. Write your own letter to Juliet to read to the group. For anonymity's sake, ask the group members to type their letters and put them into a bowl to be selected at random. Briefly discuss the letter and provide a group response.

3. Have each group member name a travel destination s/he might go to in order to learn more about love, then ask to explain his/her reasoning. Why did s/he choose this place and why is it so evocative? If the group is able to reach a consensus, take a trip together to a nearby place to do some reflecting and talking in a new setting.

Author Q&A

The book ends on a happy note, but it still begs the question: What is your current relationship status? If we are to judge from your social media accounts, you are still together and happy.

Yes, things are great. This really is the best relationship of my life. Desiree and I travel often. In fact, we were just in Verona for another visit, and we managed to see almost everyone mentioned in the book. They're all doing well too. And as the epilogue suggests, Desiree and I go to Mexico (and other warm places) in the gloom of the Canadian winter. She surfs and works on documentary films. I'm building up the courage to start another book. We support each other and both of our lives are the better for it. She's the best thing that has ever happened to me.

Was it at all hard revisiting your relationship and feelings for Claire while laying them bare for readers? Is there any type of relationship left with Claire?

It was tremendously difficult. Those are very painful memories. I thought long and hard about even wanting to write about them, but I thought if I'm going to write a book about love, then I need to be honest about everything. Of course, when I began the book, I had no idea what was waiting for me, but once it happened, I knew it had to be in the book. It would be a complete sham if I left that out. Unfortunately, Claire and I barely talk anymore. She has her life and I have mine, but I do want to be very clear that I wish her loads of happiness in the life she's chosen. I believe I said that in the acknowledgments. I'm quite worried that she'll be hurt by this book, but this certainly was not my intention. I've done everything I can to protect her privacy while still being able to tell the story. I know she'll be a great mother to her son. I know that and respect that. Maybe someday we can be friends again. I'd like that. But it will take time, probably years, and I guess that's how it has to be.

Was the structure of the book—alternating between your personal story and travels, the classroom, and research about the nature of love—one you envisioned from the outset? Or was it something that happened organically, weaving itself together as you wrote?

Ha. I often say now that about halfway through the writing, I realized that I wasn't writing this book anymore, this book was writing me. My agent was phoning me almost every week, asking, "What's happening now? My God, what's happening now?" I couldn't possibly have predicted what took place. I had no idea at all of the calamitous events awaiting me when I first had the idea to go to Verona and answer letters. And of course I had no idea about Desiree. If you must, call it star-crossed. I'm just saying that I couldn't possibly have planned any of this. This was the surprise of a lifetime.

Writing about a topic as broad and universal as love had to be a daunting task. Were there any such moments that felt that way? As a writer, what was your process for synthesizing such a big theme?

I looked at a tremendous amount of research on love before I began to write. Initially I thought I'd include a lot more of it in the book, but the story sort of took over and the research largely got left behind. Still, it gave me a grounding and an overview. I think for me, there was always that . . . well, tension is not the right word, but push and pull between synthesizing the research and the very real things that were happening to me (and what was happening to the hundreds of people whose letters I answered). I guess all of it was also wrapped around Shakespeare's exquisite story too, something I knew inside and out from my long years of teaching. In the end, it all came together: all the pieces of the puzzle fit, and I do think that I was given a real answer about love. I hope something of that comes through in the pages of this book. I hope that every reader will find part of his or her own answer in this book.

Any advice for teachers about bringing Shakespeare into the classroom? What did you find that worked well to engage students? What caused them to tune out?

Shakespeare is meant to be acted, not read. I think that's key. A line-by-line analysis is dead boring, even if Shakespeare did produce some of the greatest writing in the English language. More than anything else, Shakespeare is meant to be seen and heard. I never had the students read silently on their own; we always read it together—out loud, sometimes even in a Scottish accent. We analyzed the films too, acting as film critics. We looked at how texts can be adapted and what decisions directors make in filming. I think all of that is important in today's world. We live in a media culture, and I wanted the students to have some familiarity with how films are put together, what works emotionally and what does not. And of course they were at the age when sex and love is predominant in their brains, so it wasn't really that hard to get their attention with *Romeo and Juliet*. I'd like to think there were takeaway points, things they could apply to their own lives. And that is pretty much why Shakespeare is so great. His stories and his words really do transcend time and place. He really does speak to what's human in all of us.

While you are teaching *Romeo and Juliet*, you have to handle the fact that one of your students is being thrust into an arranged marriage. What was it like having classroom discussions on the power of love and the sacredness of marriage, but then realizing that it's not always a possibility for others in some cultures? Do you regret involving yourself?

For most of my career as a teacher, I worked at a high school that was incredibly diverse in terms of the students' cultures and language groups.

I'd done a MA in sociolinguistics, so I was always fascinated by different mind-sets and how those are encoded in language or clothing or, yes, even different ideas concerning sex and marriage. We spoke openly in class about all of this. The story of the girl in the arranged marriage was absolutely true (though of course I can't say anything about the actual student it happened to, only that her name wasn't Sadia), and the situation did end the way it ended in the book. We were also lucky to have at that school some tremendous outside resources—cultural interpreters (not just translators) who worked with families and, yes, in that particular year, a social worker who specialized in working with immigrant families. It might not have turned out that way if these people had not been in place. I just drew on their resources.

Were there any other Shakespeare plays that you enjoyed teaching? Why? Just for fun and purely hypothetically, could you see a project similar to *Juliet's Answer* based upon another Shakespeare work?

I taught a few other Shakespeare plays—although not every semester, not like *Romeo and Juliet*. I did also teach (and love) *Macbeth*, and yes, I've toyed with the idea of writing about that. It would involve not love, but aggression and ambition and assassination, and I'm not sure I'm ready to take that on. I also loved *Hamlet* and taught it many times. There's no doubt in my mind that it is the single greatest work of literature in the English language. There, I've said it. The soliloquys of Hamlet (and not just the famous one) are pure genius. There's no other way to put it.

Are you at all in touch with the Secretaries of Juliet? It appears that you were in Verona in September 2016. If so, what was it like to be back?

Yes, absolutely. They are all thrilled about this book. As I mentioned, Desiree and I were just back in Verona. Among other things, we filmed interviews with Giovanna and Manuela and Anna (and Elena, who was mentioned only briefly in the book, but who has been working there for a long time). We asked them very simply what they had learned from answering all these letters over the years. You have to think that they may be among the world's leading experts on love because of this experience, and they really did have some wonderful wisdom to impart. Look for the video. We'll post it shortly.

It was lovely to be back in Verona again. It really is a beautiful ancient city, with so many things to see. I know I'll be back again and again and again.

You have done some extensive travel writing throughout your career. How was this project different than previous assignments? Any advice for aspiring travel writers?

In my previous books, I basically wrote about a different place in each chapter (drumming in Ghana or lost languages in the Amazon, so many things). I covered a lot of ground. *Juliet's Answer* was the first time I wrote an entire book based in a single city, but what a remarkable city it is. I think my advice for aspiring travel writers would be not to write about the place so much as to write about the stories of the place or, better yet, write about the people you meet there and the stories they tell you. I can say that this is true of all of my books. I always seem to run into the most amazing people, and their experiences and stories and insights, not mine, make the writing great. You need to see the place through their eyes. That's how you get closest to the truth of a place.

What three tips would you offer to the lovelorn?

Wow, that's a difficult one. I think, though, I would say first: Be hopeful. Love will come again. I think one of the secretaries said it best when she said that you must look after yourself. You must love yourself first and then others can and will follow your example. It's not easy when you're heartbroken, but you must pick yourself up. Go do the things you love to do. Be with yourself. Find your bliss, as they say, and you'll be surprised at what happens. I have no doubt that what's most attractive to people is not looks at all. It's happiness. It's confidence. It's being okay with who you are and what you have to offer the world.